THE MANY HATS
of a WOMAN
RAFAELA BARBOUR

PENDIUM
PUBLISHING HOUSE

514-201 Daniels Street
Raleigh, NC 27605

For information, please visit our Web site at
www.pendiumpublishing.com

PENDIUM Publishing and its logo are registered trademarks.

The Many Hats of a Woman
by Rafaela Barbour

ISBN: 978-0-9816883-2-9

Printed in the United States of America

Table of Content

Dedication

This book is dedicated to my parents Hilda and James McEachin (both deceased). Thank you for the love that both of you wonderful people have provided to me and the respect that you had for me so that I could give you in return and to others. Thank you for just being there through all of my ruff and good times. Thank you for letting me grow into a beautiful woman.

To my brother James Jr., with a brother like you who would want another. To my niece Stephanie, "What up project chic?" – The one that got the gangster side of me. To my nephew James Jr. III, you will always be my little Chris Brown. To my first niece Victoria, my identical twin as you read this book. Just don't let these situations become a part of your life. You are young, gifted and Black & Puerto Rican. Keep doing what you are doing. To Milagros, my sister-in-law, thank you for blessing me with my nieces and nephew.

To Michelle, my mother-in-law (deceased), thank you for your love and support through our ruff times. To my son Devon, thank you for being a part of my life. To my best friend Karen "Rosie" Muller (deceased) for not letting out my secrets, keeping me and that crazy ass man together, and maintaining my hopes and dreams. To my God Children Jhameek (deceased) and Jhanee, I love the both of you and know that you are always in my heart.

To my other half, my husband Willis "Anthony" Barbour (a.k.a."Dee Nice" or "Master Dee"), without you putting me through all of these changes in life I could not have written this book. Thank you for the good and the bad. I will always love you.

To my "sister" in the Financial Department of MCU, Murraya

Williams, keep your head up. I love you. To my cousin Clarissa Cloud, with all of the struggles we've been through in life you always say, "Fita, you will be fine. You are fighter." Thank you for always believing in me. To Sean Cloud, thank you for keeping my cousin happy for all of these years.

To Teresa Smith-Morilla, Tiffany, Bam, Nico, and Parris, thank you for the love you've given me. To the Major Family, thank you for my Sunday dinners. They were great -love ya! To my sister in Christ Monique, thank you for your spiritual guidance. To Sandra McDaniel, thank you for believing in me through all you have watched me go through. To Extreme Vision (EV), thank you for being in my life when you didn't even know how much I was going through. I will be EV for life - from Hypnotic to EV Truck Club.

Acknowledgments

First and foremost I would like to thank GOD for the Glory is his, for giving me the strength and courage on revealing my testimonies. Ms Victoria McEachin for editing my book without changing my words. Mr. Kevin Romero for allowing me to use him as my model. Mr. Keith Harris for taking the photo. Pendium Publishing for leasing my testimony under your submission. To the people that support me through the years and for the encouragement that they have given me.

For my reader if you need to would like to contact me please do so at
Myspace.com//rafaelamceachin
Blackplanet.com//rafaelabarbour

THE MANY HATS
of a WOMAN

Chapter I

The Intellgence-1995

C-95 Riker Island

It was a little chapel setting with Jesus Christ on the cross, Mary Joseph, and Paul the disciple. The small pulpit occupied a pastor who stood in front of my future husband to be Mr. Willis "Anthony" Barbour and myself Ms. Rafaela "Fita" McEachin. We both had the look of love in our eyes, waiting to be announced husband and wife, until death do us part. This was a perfect time for marriage since Anthony and I had been dating since 1986, at least we thought it was a good idea.

The summer of August 1986, I was working for the Board of Education-Division of School Safety. It was Saturday and I was with my girlfriend Annette, a.k.a. Nette, who worked for Corrections. We were two good girls living in a bad world. We both had good jobs but were attracted to boys that lived bad lives. Not that we were saints but we both had jobs that enforced the law and our men broke the law, especially mine.

This particular Saturday was one of the last weekends of the summer and of course we where trying to enjoy those weekends before fall hit and later snow. We were hanging out where I lived at the time, Crescent St. off of Fulton St. in Brooklyn N.Y. Nette and I was driving on the South Conduct towards Queens where I exited on 150 St. off of the Belt Parkway. We had no particular destination, we were just driving. I decided to get off of the Belt Parkway because there was a

1986 black Maxima off on the side of the street. The car had smoke
seeping from the front of the hood so Nette said, "Go see if they need
help." You know when you are with your girlfriends they always try
to gas you up so that you build enough confidence to confront a guy;
that's just what Nette did to me. We pulled over and approached the guy
in my electric blue Buick Sky-Hawk and motioned the passenger
window downward and I said to one of the two guys, "You need help?"
The fine dark skinned guy with plenty of jewelry on his neck and
diamond rings, wearing a valor Fila sweat suit with Fila sneakers said,
"No thank you." I replied, "You sure you don't need a boost?" The dark
skinned guy said, "No" so that's when Nette and I pulled off and went on
our Saturday adventure into the borough of Queens.

On our way back to catch the Conduit going north, we saw the
same car parked in the same position. I decided that Nette and I should
go ask again if the guys needed help. "Do you need some assistance?" I
said sarcastically. The dark skinned guy replied "You could take us to
Baisley Projects." I quickly said, "Okay" but had no clue where Baisley
was and how to get there. The two guys hopped in the back seat of my
car and I drove off. The dark skinned guy instantly directed me to our
destination in order to get us there in a timely fashion. We flirted and he
tried to kick it to me. He later asked for my telephone number. Just as I
was passing him my number, we arrived to the projects and the dark
skinned guy immediate jumped out of the car telling me to hand my
number to his friend, so I did. I did not understand why he did not take
it himself but I figured that maybe he was in a rush to find someone to
help fix his car that was still along side the road in Queens. Once the
light skinned guy got out of the car, I took off. I realized afterward I
didn't even get either of their names. My main focus was on the dark
skinned guy while Nette conversed with his friend. Nonetheless, I don't
know what I was thinking letting two strangers into my car.

About two weeks passed and I arrived home from work. My
father said, "Fita, someone by the name of Anthony called." I said,
"Who?" My father said, "Anthony" and I replied, "I don't know any
Anthony." My father said, "Well someone you gave the damn number to
said he will call back." "Okay! Thanks daddy," I replied. "If you stop
giving the number out to whomever then you would know who it is that
calls," said my father.

A few hours went by and the telephone rang. It was about 6:30
p.m. when my father yelled, "Fita, it's Anthony again." So it was my
time to find out who the hell was Anthony. I picked up the phone and
said, "Hello!" The guy on the other end said, "Hi, is this Fita?" I said,
"Yes" with a confused look on my face. The guy said, "This is Anthony.

We met about two weeks ago. Remember, the black Maxima?" My eyes lit up. I said, "Hi...!" I was very glad to hear from him. I asked, "And the car?" Anthony said, "My car is fine." "What was wrong with it?" I asked. Anthony replied, "Nothing." I said, "Why was it smoking that way?" He said, "Just to let you know this is not Premo, this is the one that was suppose to pass your number to him." At that moment, I was quiet. I hesitated for a second but then said, "What up Anthony?" He then said, "Well I didn't give him the number. He doesn't deserve a girl like you." I said, "And you do?" He said, "Premo has three children in the same project you dropped us off at, so you already know where that's going. I said, "Oh! Okay. Thanks for the info." He said, "Do you have a man?" I said, "No." "Do you go out on dates?" he asked and I said, "Yes." He continued, "Do you do movies?" and I said, "Yes." And at the moment is when Anthony asked me on our first date in which I agreed to. After confirming the date, we stayed on the telephone for a few more minutes then we said good night.

I worked a full week but anticipated seeing Anthony on Saturday, especially since I had forgotten what he had looked like being that Premo was a fine dark skinned brother who initially caught me eye. I really didn't pay much attention to Anthony. My girl Nette was engaged in more of a conversation with him while in the car. Saturday came and I was getting myself ready to meet Anthony. He was picking me up at 7:00 p.m. The phone rung and I immediately got nervous. My dad said, "It's for you Fita!" I said, "Okay daddy. I got it." So I picked up the phone and there was Anthony, "Are you ready?" "Yes," I said and he replied, "Come down stairs." Before I went downstairs, I decided to look out of the window and my dad followed (Oh! did my father look mad). He shouted, "What kind of work he do?" Anthony had rolled up in a flashy gold Jaguar that shimmered in the light. As I began to head out of the door, I told my dad that I would explain to him later. When I walked out of my house, Anthony got out of the car so that he could open the door for me. I acted as if I was not impressed but I really was. He said, "What would you like to do? Go and eat first or go to the movies?" I said, "Let's do the movies first." But once we arrived to the movie theatre, I realized that that was a bad idea because we talked through the whole movie. By the time we went to eat, we were very relaxed with each other, kissing each other on the cheek and chin. We laughed and joked about how we met. It turned out to be a very good night. After dinner, Anthony dropped me off home.

Following our first date, Anthony and I talked on the phone for weeks, and hours at a time. We had so much in common such as we both were Gemini's, both had birthdays in June (his was the 11th and mine on the 5th), we liked the same music, and when it balled down to it we wanted the same things in life – to be successful, successful, successful! Since our first date, it was the beginning of a great love affair. It didn't bother me that I was older than him by two years. At the time, I was 23 years of age and didn't look a day over 18, and he was 21 years old.

"Time waits for no one." It had now been three months that I was in a relationship with Anthony and I was working at Prospect Heights High School. Everyday, Anthony would meet me after work and we use to have so much fun together. Of course we flirted and kissed, we were always together, when time allowed and he wasn't taking care of "business." It was always about me. You know what they say, "What you say and do in the dark comes out in the light."

January 1987, it was time for me to be re-assigned to another school as part of my job so my new assignment was at George Westinghouse H.S. in Brooklyn N.Y. It was Monday morning at George Westinghouse H.S., my first day on the job, and I was at the main entrance where I was checking student programs and school identification cards as the students entered the high school. While at my post, I scanned the crowed to see how many people were on line to enter the school and someone immediately caught my eye. It was Anthony on the line to get into the school. He did not notice me. As he got closer to the doorway where I was standing, I said, "Program card or ID young man." He quickly looked up as he noticed a familiar voice and our eyes met. It was shocking for the both of us but even more embarrassing for me. As he handed me his program card, I could have died. I grabbed his card and instantly got sick. I needed a break. I needed to think of what I was going to do. How was I going to break it off? How could I have gotten involved with a student? How could I not have known? All kinds of thoughts were running through my mind. I started thinking about my job. This is fraternizing; this is the first thing addressed in the School Safety training. How could I have fallen in love with a student, an eighteen year old boy. This young handsome man, who knew exactly what to do with a woman, bamboozled me. He knew what to do, what to say, what buttons to touch, what sides to rub, and how to kiss. He would put me in my glory, but it had to be over. When the crowd lessened and the majority of the students were in the school building, I went outside to make sure none of the doors were unlocked or propped open with papers (the usual routine of students trying to sneak in and out of school). While outside, I lit a cigarette so it would help calm me down so I could situate my thoughts. All I could think about was the fact that he straight up lied. That fine, husky, cock-diesel, dress to impress, pockets stacked with cash, young man was a student. What was I going to do? This was a man that I had spent the last four months getting to know and I liked everything about him. We were great together. I felt stuck. Even though we didn't have sex yet, I sure as hell want him to be inside of me like yesterday.

It was time to dismiss the students for the day and I had spent the whole day in the security room with a headache so the other security officer covered for me. After dismissal, it was time for me to leave. It was time for me to beep (page) the liar. The phone rang back instantly and I picked up and said, "Anthony, HOW COULD YOU?" He said, "First of all, everything went so fast. I wanted to tell you. But at the time that we met, you were working at Prospect Heights and I didn't think that there was a need to tell you. But when you told me that you got re-assigned, I didn't think it was a good time then because we were already mentally involved and I didn't think it mattered. We had already started to bond." His sexy voice soothed my soul. As a result of our conversation, I decided to keep him as my man and played it by ear, and prayed on it.

The next few days was kind of ruff. The both of us being in the same building were kind of hard to get use to. Anthony was a senior but he knew everybody in the building, even my co-workers in security. As I observed him, it was like he had everyone under his control. The man was smooth with his surrounding. Third period began and my post was at the cafeteria. Typically, lunch was where stuff always started between students and with me. I was located at the doorway of the cafeteria and I would observe all of the young girls all up in my man's face but I acted as if I didn't see what was happening. Besides, I was young and fine myself, and there were always other men and students hitting on me, which use to always piss Anthony off. He would always say, "I don't think your father is going to like that McEachin." This was the signal that he was getting upset.

This behavior went on everyday but I believed this was helpful for our relationship because it was a way to learn about one another and how to deal with this type of situation since we both were good looking and people were going to hit on us all the time. Besides we were compatible. However, after a while, Anthony started getting jealous and he would be up under me a lot more in the cafeteria. But people didn't think once that I was his girl, he had everyone in the school thinking that I was his father's girlfriend.

About seven months went by and Anthony said that he needed to speak to me (it was very important). Therefore, I said we could talk about it at home but he said no so I took him to the side of the hall as if I was disciplining him within the school building. Anthony said, "It is not the time to play games about dating. You are my girl so it's time to act like it." I said, "What are talking about?" He said, "One of the other men in the building was speaking to me about how they would love to hit it (have sex with me) so I think you should stop joking with the men here." I said, "Okay but we both are two of biggest flirts in the building. What's up with you?" He said nothing. I went on to say, "Is it that you are insecure cause I didn't even give you none (sex). He said, "You are damn right and I know that you have been with no one but me day in and day out so it's time." Of course that was the beginning of heavy sex conversation; this was the topic of every conservation after that point. Anthony would say, "When are we going to have sex? When are you going to let me cum inside of you?" Every night I would get wet talking to Anthony. Although I enjoyed our sex conversations, on the other hand, I felt like I needed to talk about all the things he wanted to talk.

The next day, Anthony started to act differently. He came up close to me and started whispering in my ear. The change in his body language triggered one of his boys to say, "Yo Dee! You sure that's your father's girl? Or is that your girl?" That's the day Anthony let our secret out and told his friend Half-Pint I was his girl. From that day forward, Half-Pint respected me in a totally different way. Half said to me, "I knew that it was more between the two of you then what you told people in the building cause I use to bust Dee giving you a lot of money in the cafeteria. I knew both of you would say it was for his father but I knew better." After that day, all of Dee's people in the school knew about me and him, Spanish Eli from Far Rockaway, Raheem, and especially all of the guys that worked for him.

Now that everyone knew, I kind of felt special. I felt even more connected to Dee now that his friends knew but I was still scared. I was a little bit scared of where the relationship was going, especially whether or not it was time to have sex with him. The way I was feeling, I wondered if it would be sex to him or making love since I felt like I was falling in love. Would he feel the same? Would it be making love or just sex to him?

It was the beginning of April and the weather was just beginning to warm up. Anthony asked me if I would go with him clubbing (out to a night club) and I said, "No." He then asked me to go with him to the movies and I said, "No." I kept on saying no because for me it was different when I met Anthony. Although we went to the movies, dinner, clubbing, and hung out at the park, people didn't know about us. Our situation had since changed. I didn't know if I was going to run into a student from the school or one of my co-workers so it was intense.

Instead, we decided to meet on Cross Bay Blvd next to White Castle so that we could chill. Most of the students that went to Westinghouse lived In Brooklyn. I jumped on the A train and shot-out to Queens. When I arrived to my destination, Dee was wearing Fila hoodie and he was looking fine as ever. I slowly got out of my vehicle to greet him. After we kissed, we immediately began walking but I noticed that Dee wasn't walking towards White Castle, he passed it and was going towards the end of the block. I finally realized what he was walking towards, a motel. It was the Cross Bay End Motel. I just laughed inside because I knew what was about to happen and I was okay with it because I wanted it to happen.

Before we entered the motel building, Anthony asked me if I wanted something to eat from the pizza shop. I said yes so we purchased a pizza, some soda and beer, and headed to the hotel. Anthony had already reserved the room and checked in before we met up with each other so we made our way directly to the room with no interruptions. As we entered the room, I began to feel uneasy. It wasn't because I did not want to be with him, it's because I had never been in a motel before and I always thought that motels where for "hoe's" (women that you don't take home to your mother). As I walked into the room, it was a big and was divided into a bedroom and a living room with a bathroom in the corner, it was cute. There were two night stands and a big dresser with a television on top, and pictures on the wall. Anthony put the pizza down on the table and I put the soda and beer down as well and that was all she wrote. I never got to eat or drink until our session was over. We laid down on the bed and Anthony removed my clothes and I removed his.

Anthony was gentle, kind, and patient. As he kissed me, his hands caressed my breast. While he attempted to go down on me, he slowly kissed my breast and played with my "bell button" and as he licked me all over, he asked me to touch is nine-inch friend. I did just that. He asked, "Are you ready?" I replied, "YES!" and he slowly entered me from the side. Tears began to roll down my cheeks. I knew that this was a turning point in my life and our relationship. I knew we could never go back to being just friends and that it would be different while in each other's presence at Westinghouse. The time with each other was intense, so intense that Anthony even screamed my name. It was like he had been waiting so long for this to happen and at that moment he was able to release it all and was now able to breathe again. Of course I called his name too. He was the best I had ever had. There was only one man that I had ever been with before Anthony but Anthony was better.

It was now Saturday morning and we had to separate. I had to go home and so did Anthony, well he had to go check on his money.

We went the whole day without speaking to each other. On Sunday afternoon, he called me. We spoke but it was as if nothing had ever happened. To me that was great. However, we did talk about if we were happy with the sex results and yes we where. Love making was another thing that made us compatible.

Monday morning, the first day back after a long pleasant weekend of engaging in love with each other, I was at my post at the main desk near the front door, waiting for the students to show their ID's. Anthony rolled up on me and said, "Good morning Ms. McEachin!" I said "Good morning Mr. Barbour" and all of the officers looked as though they thought Anthony was being sarcastic. Therefore, one of the officer's said, "What's that all about?" I said, "His father must have spoke to him because I told his father that he was getting a little bit beside himself in school." The officer replied, "That's right! So officer McEachin knows your father Dee?" Anthony shook is head and said, "Yeah!"

Third period, I was back at the cafeteria as usual and so was Dee, Half, and his other peoples. As I walked around the cafeteria, I noticed a young lady named Debra towards the back of the cafeteria. I remembered checking her program card and it did indicate that that was her lunch period. There was something strange about her. I couldn't put my finger on it at that moment. I began walking to the table where she was sitting and she said, "McEachin!" and I said, "Yes Debra! What up?" She asked, "So you are Dee's father's girl?" and I said, "Yes." Debra went on to say, "Well how can I get with your son? I've been checking him out for about a year. I am ready to give him some good and plenty love-in." I was shocked ("cat had my tongue"). I said, "What?" She said, "I want to give him some this candy." I said, "I don't know. Have you ever talked to him?" Debra replied, "Yes. But he keeps telling me he has a girl." I said, "Well Debra, you have to respect that" and I walked away. I had to get away from her because I could have broken her neck or cursed her out about trying to get with my man.

It was getting crazy now. All the young girls felt like they could confide in me about what they were feeling about Dee, not knowing that I was his girl. They kept on coming to me about Dee because everyone was convinced that I was his father's girlfriend. When the girls were trying to get at him, they would tell me because I was considered the cool officer. I was "down with the program." Nine months into the relationship and we were going strong, now more then ever, Anthony said, "I want you to meet my mother." I was afraid. "What was she going to say about me being older then you Anthony?" I asked. "She's okay with it. I talk about you all the time. She doesn't believe that you are that much older than me anyway. She says when you speak to her, you sound very young," he replied.

Chapter II

The Award Money

Saturday night, June 11th, 1987, Anthony's birthday, was the night that I was going to meet his mother. I have never forgotten this day. I was so embarrassed. As we approached the door of Anthony's house and placed the key in the key hole to open it, his uncle immediately said, "What up Ant? What up Fita?" I was shocked. Anthony's uncle and I were in the same class in junior high school. His uncle said, "You're dating my nephew?" My eyes went down to the floor and I shook my head. We then walked further into his home and his mother said, "So you were in my brother's class?" and I said, "Yes." Anthony's mother Michelle said, "Well, you will teach my son how to treat a woman. You are welcome here anytime" and I said, "Thank you!" She added, "There's one thing I don't play around with here," said Michelle. "What's that?" I said. Michelle said, "I am the only woman in that shower and getting up early in the morning leaving this house." Basically, Michelle was telling me not to think about spending the night because if I got caught leaving in the morning, it was going to be problems. I let her know that I understood. "Enjoy your stay!" she said. Anthony was embarrassed but his mother was real and I liked that. Following our encounter with his mother, we went to his room where his baby brother was. Dee introduced me to him. His name was Teron. After the introduction, Teron knew it was time to leave the room and it was just Anthony and I. That night, we watched a movie and his mother made us dinner. When we got back to his room, Anthony decided to take out his two turn tables and all the d.j. equipment that his father bought him. He decided to play a slow jam by Atlantic Star. As the song played, Anthony began to undress me until I was fully nude then he undressed himself. It was on! He entered inside of me for the second time. For me, it seemed like forever since our first intimate encounter but it was worth the wait. It was better than the first. After we finished, it was about 11:30 p.m. when we decided to leave so that he could drop me off home. His mother was asleep and so was everyone else in the house.

A couple of weeks went by and we started to spend a lot more evenings together. It got as bad as I was always stayed at his house but left around 1:30 a.m. There were a bunch of sleepless nights. One day, I spent the night and I had to sneak out of the house. It was a weekday so I had to go straight to work, and Anthony had to go to school. This was the beginning of danger. Knowing that we were getting out of the same bed together and we were going to the same building where I worked and he went to school, how could I have lost control? Why did I stay with him? As I was trying to sneak out, Ms. Michelle said, "Fita, is that you leaving my house at this time in the morning?" I put my head down and said, "Yes." She said, "You remember my conversation?" and I said, "Yes." "Don't you have and explain" said Michelle. I looked at her in her eyes and I said, "No Ms. Barbour. It's just that I was very tired when I came to see your son yesterday and I over slept. He didn't put the alarm on for me to leave." She looked at me and said, "You are not a child. You are a woman and I respect that you didn't lie to me. Now get your butt to work." She hugged me and I left with a smile.

It was Monday and I was running late as a result of getting caught by Anthony's mother. I ran up to the locker room to change into my uniform and as I walked by the principle's office, the principle said that he wanted to see me when I got dressed. When he said that, my mind went racing. For a moment, I thought Anthony may have said something. As I walked downstairs, the principal said to me that he wanted me to get a hold of Mr. Hamburger, another nickname of Anthony's. Before I got to Westinghouse, Anthony apparently used to threaten students and take their hamburgers in the cafeteria so people started calling him hamburger. I asked the principal if something was wrong and he said, "Yes, he had a fight this morning and I want to get to the bottom of it." I proceeded to look for Anthony but I could not find him so I decided to beep him. He called back instantly on the security phone line at the main entrance. I whispered to him, "Where are you?" He said, "I had to leave." "Why?" I asked. "I'll tell you when you get home" and he hung up the phone. I went to the principle and told him that I had looked all over for Hamburger but I couldn't find him anywhere. The principal said, "Well if you see his father, tell him if I can't get this quashed soon his son will not be able to enter the school" and I replied, "Okay." So here I was, the love of my life was in trouble and I had just woke up in his bed sneaking out of his house and went to work and now he was on the run from school officials. What more could happen today? As the day ended, Anthony called me again and asked me to go to his house and I told him, "You have no idea what happened to me when you left me in the bed and as I was sneaking out your mother caught me. I don't think I'm ready for another lecture." Anthony laughed and said, "Just come to my house." I told him that I had to go to my house first because I had to face my mother and father and hear their long lecture and get it over with. He said ok and we both laughed. I went on home that evening to get cursed out by my parents and of course my father was breaking about how he would not been surprised if he found me in the river because of the dangerous life I had gotten myself into. My dad knew that my man was into the drug game and all the problems that surrounded him would eventually affect me. My father should have understood where I was coming from being that he raised me in that same kind of life. But you know those kinds of fathers; he wanted better for his daughter and didn't want his son involved in it either. My mother just counseled me on my behavior. She understood that I was living her life. She remembered the day she met my father. She didn't want the same life for me but she knew that she could not have been convinced otherwise back in her day. She wanted the man that she wanted, which happened to be my father. The game might have been different back then but it is what it is today. After all this time, they still never knew that Anthony was a student where I worked. That information would have probably torn them apart. It was a dangerous game I was playing so I had to be cautious. I stayed home that evening. It was too much for me to soak in the fact that I got caught, got to work late, had to search for Hamburger, got home and got screamed on by my parents. It was just too much for one day so I just took a shower and laid down. I decided to call my man and talk to him until I was tried. We decided that we would get together on Tuesday. That was the longest Monday of my life.

On Tuesday, I went on to work, of course I was at my post checking for program cards and ID's, but for some reason I didn't see Anthony so I beeped him. It was now third period and he still hadn't called me back. I began to get worried. I decided to call his house and his mother picked up and put me on hold while she went to go check to see if he was still in his room. She said, "I guess he went to school" and I said, "Okay." It was about 1:00 p.m. when he called me back. I asked, "What took you so long calling me back?" He said, "I had too take care of some business. Do you mind?" and I said, "No!" What up with the principal looking for you?" I asked. He said, "Oh! I had to put some people in check in the building." I said, "So you gonna' talk to the principal?" He said "Yeah. I'll be there tomorrow" and I said, "Okay." Anthony replied, "You know we have to talk so come to my house today" and I agreed.

When I hung up the telephone, it was the end of the day and it was time to get off of my shift at work and into the danger zone. I got on the train to get to Anthony's house. I was trying to figure out what he had to speak to me about but I could not come up with a solution so I left it alone until I got there. As the train approached the station of Beach 98, my heart started to pound because I had not been there since Ms. Barbour had caught me sneaking out. I was scared to face her. I walked into the building and there were two girls in front, a black girl and white girl but they said nothing to me so I rung the bell and the door opened. I decided to walk up the stairs instead of waiting for the elevator and as I got to the door and rung the bell, Anthony opened the door and said hi baby. I replied baby hello. I asked, "Where is your mother?" He said, "She went to Brooklyn to see my father." I got comfortable and Anthony began to explain to me that business was not doing well and that's why he has to stay out of school. He later went onto say that he had to go out of town on Friday. I asked why and he said that one of the businesses out of town was having trouble. I just sat there and looked at him and said "You going to mess up in school for the street life?" He looked at me and said, "Before you, it was this and now it's you and this." I looked at him and said okay. Then he looked at me with a tear and he said, "I might have to do 8 months in prison." I was stunned. I looked at him and I started to cry. He said, "Stop being a punk. I worked hard and I thought you could handle whatever comes with this business." I looked and said, "What do you want me to do?" He said, "Nothing. Just take care of my mother and brothers and I said okay. I promised to do what I could. He then handed me a brown bag and said, "I don't expect you to help support them but use this wisely." When I opened the bag, there lied a bank card and set of car keys. I didn't know what to say or do. I just took it and put it in my pocket-book. We decided to stay in the house and reminisced about the time we met and the dangerous things that we did. He asked me if I knew how to cook fish and I said yes so we went to the store and bought fish. As I cooked the fish, we made love in the kitchen. He lifted me on the kitchen counter and he was inside of me. I asked him to promise to never leave me.

It was now about 11:00 p.m., and it was time for me to get home. I did not want to hear my parents screaming at me again so I said, "Baby, it's time that I leave" and he asked, "Why?" "Anthony, you know why." He said, "Spend the night." I said, "Your mother will kill me." "No, she's good with you. I don't know what you said or what you did but my mother likes you a whole lot and I told her that after I tell you that I would want to spend more time with you before I go to Delaware so she agreed that it would be okay." So he convinced me to stay but I still had to call my parents and tell them that I was staying at Anthony's house. Here we go again, the lecture. They said, "We will speak to you tomorrow!" At about 12:00 a.m., Ms. Barbour arrived home with the boys and that's when I met Raymond. He was the middle brother. I've now met all Anthony's siblings from both his parents. He had other brothers and sisters but I had not met them yet (they were from his father's second marriage). Ms. Barbour said, "I hope that you two cooked dinner" and I replied, "Yes." "You cooked for this boy?" asked Ms. Barbour and I said yes excitingly. She said, "I smell fish." "That's what I cooked." "Girl, that boy loves seafood. You are in trouble," said Ms. Barbour. We both laughed and she said good night and she went to put the boys to sleep.

We went back to his room to lie down. He started looking at me, touching my face and kissing my neck. As Anthony kissed my neck, I held him tight and then I got on top of him and I sat up on his package and road him like a pony for the rest of the night until morning when he screamed my name. I knew that he was in his glory. It was time to get some sleep because I had to be at work for 7:30 a.m. He was going to school to speak to the principal (the day of the jury with Mr. Hamburger and the Principal). I was at the main door and Anthony was entering the school building. Before I could say anything, one of my co-workers escorted Anthony to the principal's office. By the time I looked up, it was a 10-13, that means that there was a fight so I had to run to assist the other officers. All I saw was some of the students running in the direction of the principal's office. As I got closer, I saw Anthony swinging his fist towards a guy. I didn't know what to do so I went towards Anthony and I noticed that his fist was not going to stop. I was not going to get hit. After he punched the guy out, Anthony ran out of the building.

Anthony was in some real trouble now. Not only did he punch the guy, but he had busted the honor roll glass case in the hallway that housed the names of each student to recognize their achievements in the city wide exams. Now there was a new charge on Anthony. He would be charged with assault and reckless endangerment to school property; that was an automatic suspension for Anthony. It was time for his parents to have a meeting with the principal before he could attend any more classes. It was more drama in my life because Anthony's mother didn't know that I had worked at the high school. She only knew that his girl was an older woman, not that I was a staff member at the high school. Here comes trouble.

Being that "I knew his father," school officials asked me to contact his father or mother to set up a meeting at the high school. I didn't tell Anthony what I had been ordered to do since I knew that he was going out of town on Friday. Instead, I just let the day go by and allowed for Anthony to cool off. He didn't need anymore stresses.

At approximately 2:00 p.m., my beeper went off and I looked at the number, which didn't look familiar to me. When I got a chance, I called the number back and it was Anthony calling me to find out if I was alright. He thought I may have gotten hit during the fight. I told him I was fine and that I ducked and missed any punches coming my way. At that time, I told him that the principal requested to see his mother before he would be allowed back in school. I also informed him that he is suspended until then. He said, "Okay, but you know that I'm leaving tomorrow to Delaware?" I said, "I thought you were leaving on Friday?" "Well, if I can't go to school then I might as well go sooner so that I could take care of my business. You know you have to come and see me before I leave," said Anthony. I told him that I would see him after I got off of work.

At 6:30 p.m., I started to pack a bag to go to Anthony's house. I had already spoken to my mother because my father was not home. I figured I'd go home anyhow to see my family, especially my mother because I had not been spending time with her and my father was not home as a result of being a hustler in the streets. After my mother would get home from work, she would always like to see her only daughter. My brother was the younger of the two but my brother started a family at a young age and decided to marry also. All my mother had was me as a result of my brother having a wife and two beautiful children, and one more on the way. Junior had his hands tied and could not be around as much as my parents would have liked him to. But my brother and my mother spoke on the phone everyday. Regardless, we were a tight family. My brother lived in Brownville and my parents and I lived in the border line of Brooklyn and Queens. My niece and my nephew were adorable, and the third one on the way was going to be just as adorable as the other two. My sister-in-law was cool. We got along just like sisters.

Once I finished packing my overnight bag, the telephone rang. It was my daddy checking with my mother to see if I had come home. My dad wanted to speak with me. I told my father that after work I would go straight home because Anthony was going out of town to Delaware. My dad was fine with the situation and said he'd see me tomorrow "baby girl," a little nickname my father always called me. After I got off of the phone, I kissed and I hugged my mother and went on my way. When I got to Anthony's house, his mother and his brothers were in the living room watching the movie *Gremlins*. That was when Ms. Barbour said to me, "The boys tell me that they watch this move all the time but this is my first time watching it." Anthony and I laughed. Then she said, "Is it that every time I leave the boys with you two, you put the movie on and leave them so that you two can go in the room?" I was shocked. Anthony said, "No mom. That's just the movie we all like." Mom ended the conversation there and we all hung out until about 11:00 p.m. when Anthony said to me, "Thank you for just putting up with my nonsense." I said, "Thank you for just keeping a mature relationship and not taking my job." That's when he said the relationship was bigger then that and explained how he's a man not a boy, and would never rat me out so I didn't have to worry about him trying to get my job taking away from me; that wasn't his motive. I asked, "What is your motive?" He just looked at me and said, "It's not that. It's bigger than that." That's when we jumped on each other and got at it again until we fell asleep.

It was morning, and Anthony was leaving to Delaware. I was very sad because he was going to leave me for the weekend. He said, "Stop looking so sad and come up close to me." I said, "What?" "Go in your pocketbook and get the brown bag that I gave you a few days ago. Then go in my closet and get the book that is sticking out," said Anthony. So I did what he said and I sat down. I began to feel nervous for some reason. Anthony then asked me to open the book and take out the bank statement that was in it. As I searched between the pages, Anthony said "Look, if something were to happen to me, this will be a start for you and my family..." I looked at the statement and it said $65,000. "Does this say what I think it says? How could you have this kind of money in the bank?" He said, "Well it started with an accident that I had and the lawsuit money went into the bank. Then I started depositing my own cash and no one ever asked where it was coming from. Now you have my life savings. You know what's in the account but you don't know the numbers to withdraw from the account and I'm going to give that to my mother. Okay?" "Okay!" I said.

It was now time to take him to the bus terminal. I was really involved in his life so I played my part because when you love a man and he leaves you all of his earnings, nothing else mattered. In those days, was a plus. I got ready and pulled the keys out of the brown bag to the car. I went to the parking lot underneath his building and I got in the car. It was my first time driving his beautiful jaguar. I pulled up to the building and my man was ready. I took him to the bus terminal and asked him to call me once he arrived to Delaware then I went to work. I pulled up to the parking lot at my job and some of the students seen me and said, "Boy McEachin, Dee's father sure takes care of you" and I smiled and said, "Yeah he does." I walked into the school and got right to work, "Program card and ID." It was the end of the day and I had not yet heard from Anthony. I decided that I would beep him as soon as I got home. I went right home and I took my uniform off and got comfortable. Immediately after, I beeped my man. About an hour later, Anthony called back. I shouted, "Why didn't you call me when you got there?" He said, "Baby, don't get crazy. I just didn't want to brother you at work." I said, "Oh! Okay. How is everything?" "After this morning, everything is better." I didn't ask about what he meant by that because there are certain things that I didn't need to know, at least not over the telephone. I said, "Baby, when are you coming home?" "Sunday... I gotta' talk to you later." I said bye and we hung up.

The next day, I went to work and I went straight home. It was Friday evening and had no plans. I decided to go to my best friend Rosie's house. She said, "What a surprise that you are here. Why do you look so sad?" I said, "Anthony went out of town." "Oh! Know wonder you are sad." I told Rosie that I had something to speak to her about. "You are my best friend and I know you would not tell anyone until my death... He left me $65,000 and said if something were to happen to him he asked me to take care of his family." Rosie said, "WHAT?" I said, "Should I repeat it?" She said, "No...! Girl you are lying." I assured her I was telling the truth. She asked, "In cash?" I said, "No, in the bank." She said, "Let me see" so I showed her the bank statement. She couldn't believe it. She asked why I was so sad and I confessed to her that if he didn't come back I don't know if I could be happy without him. Rosie looked at me for a second and said, "Girl, you are whipped! I understand that you have such a good and dangerous time with him, and days are not the same without him, but girl you got $65,000 you should not be sad." Rosie was the only one of my friends that knew he was a student. It was 11:00 pm. and I had to go home when my beeper went off. I checked the number and it was a Delaware area code so I called from Rosie's house. After it rung two times, my man picked up and said, "Where are you mommy? You said you were not home and that you left early to Rosie's so where are you?" I said, "I'm at Rosie's. I was leaving now." Anthony said, "Okay. Let me speak to Rosie." I passed the phone to Rosie and Anthony said, "What up Rosie?" Rosie said, "Nothing. What up with you Ant?" I chimed in, "Out of town." Rosie said, "I know and that's the only time I get to see my girl." Anthony laughed and said, "When I get back we are going to make a trip there."

Rosie then asked, "Ant, do you mind if Fita take me somewhere tomorrow in your car?" He said, "Rosie, you know better than to ask. What ever you two do it's fine with me. I can't take your girl from you. You and her had been together since before I was born." We laughed and Rosie thanked him and wished him well on his trip. Rosie passed the phone back to me and Anthony said, "Baby beep me when you get home so I will know you are safe." "Okay." And that's when I said it, "I love you!" He said, "Okay" and hung up.

It was Sunday evening and my man was back home. We got together and discussed what happened on his trip. I didn't get many details out of Anthony since he seemed to talk in riddles when he did not want me to know about the nasty things he did to people and I didn't ask. We ate at the dinner table with his family, and then I decide to leave. Before I left, Anthony called me into his bedroom and asked me if I was alright. I told him yes. He said, "You can't be alright if you did not give me any loving." I looked at him and said, "Why? You want to start an episode?" He said, "I could do that. You are mine." I laughed and said, "You are hooked on the pudding." He said, "Yeah and is something wrong with that?" I assured him that it wasn't and we had our quick episode. I said, "Well you can have quickie" and he laughed. Then I said, "What's going to happen when your mother comes up?" He said, "I don't know. Oh and, I didn't get a chance to tell her that you work at the school so let's just play it by ear." That made me scared.

Monday morning I was on my post at the main door. I sat down when a women asked me where the principal's office was located. When I looked up to address the woman it was Ms. Barbour. She looked at me and was in shock. All I could do is play like nothing was wrong and politely said, "Hello!" She played along and said, "Hi! Would you direct me to the principal's office please? I'm Willis Barbour's mother and I have a meeting with the principal." I looked at her and said, "I know. We have been expecting you." My partner looked at her and she said to me, "Would you please escort me?" and I agreed. As far as my partner was concerned, he just thought that Ms. Barbour was shocked because I worked at the school that her son attended and I was dating her ex-husband. But me and Ms. Barbour knew that she was shocked because I was her son's girl and she didn't know I worked at the school. "Fita, what Is this mess?" she asked. I looked at her and said, "I can't explain it to you now but I promise I will explain it to you at your house today. Please don't be mad." She said, "You make it your business to come over today." Once I dropped Ms. Barbour off to the principal's office, I returned to my post and asked my partner to cover me for a break. I needed a cigarette badly. I was afraid that Ms. Barbour was going to blow my cover while in the principal's office. I thought that she had taken enough of the bull with me being an older woman and breaking her rule about staying over her house. Now, I worked in the school her son attended. It had to be too much for her. I was sure that it would be the end of my career. I stood outside the building, thinking about what was going to happen to me. What was I going to tell my mother? I would have had to start a new career in jail. It was statutory rape. I knew the law; I enforced it. Although School Safety, I had a police officer status. I swore into the NYC Police Department and had a gold shield to prove it. What was wrong with me? I was making too many wrong choices and God was on my side up until now but he's the only one that could save me.

When I arrived to my post, my partner said, "The principal would like to see you." I looked at her and I asked, "Now?" "Yes!" As I walked to the principal's office I prepared myself. I was ready to accept my punishment, ready to get my conduct of dismissal so that I could go wherever life took me. When I arrived, the principal asked, "McEachin would you have the pleasure of escorting Ms. Barbour out of the building and notify every officer that Mr. Barbour is to attend classes tomorrow." I said, "Yes!" (That was for God saving my butt again). I escorted Ms. Barbour out of the building, thanking her for her visit and informed her that I would see her after work. As I escorted her out the door my partner said, "Oh, she doesn't like you because you are seeing her ex-husband" and I said, "yeah something like that," as I entered the building.

I couldn't wait to get off of work so I could talk to Rosie and tell her what had happened to me today. It was always some drama and Rosie would always miss it. That's because she could no longer get out much because she just had her first child and her mother was not having that. When the day ended, I spoke to Rosie and she said, "You are such a lucky witch. You better thank your lucky stars." "I know but I have to complete my mission," which meant that I had to go and speak to Anthony's mother and would call her afterwards.

I called my mother at her job and told her that I would be getting home a little late and that Anthony would drop me off. My mother said, "Okay, I'll see you later. It was time to meet with my man's mother. Ms. Barbour was always so real with what life had to offer, but I didn't know what to expect out of her this time. As I got to her building, I was scared and nervous. She had been waiting patiently with her son Anthony. Before I could ring the bell, the door opened up and I could not have time to breath before she said, "What is going on with you and him?" I started to explain when Anthony said, "Mom it's my fault. When I met her it was summertime and lied about my age. Before she realized my real age, it was when she had already met you. But we still decided to stay together and she got re-assigned to another school and it happened to be my school but it was just too late. By that time, we were already involved mentally and were on our way to a physical adventure." Ms. Barbour looked at her son and said, "Boy, you could not have put that in a better way. I don't know what's gotten into you the last couple of months but you have changed. I don't know if it's Fita or you are just growing up but I like it." She looked at me and said, "Take care of my son." "I will." She said, "I like you and I don't know why I opened up to you but I can see that you love my son and I have to respect you for that. I know that if he needed someone to help him or his family, it would be you so I thank you for that. I can see that you come from a two parent home because you have such a bond with my son. Your mother did a great job with you and someday I would like to meet her and your father." I said, "Thank you! And one day you will meet my parents." That day took our relationship to another level.

Anthony returned back to school and it was much more refreshing. We were much more open with each other. It was like we didn't have to hide from his mother about anything. The week went by and it was now time for the first court date of his case that we had discussed for about a week now. It had something to do with some little stolen car. He was given 8 months to 1 year. He returned from court and said he needed to speak with me so we went to the cafeteria where we did most of our talking so that people weren't in our business. Anthony explained that he told the judge that he would turn himself in and they gave him a week; when he said that to me, it really hit me hard. I asked, "One week Anthony? What am I going to do?" He said, "Yeah, one week. Well you have everything I worked for so you decide" and he left. At this point, I couldn't finish my shift. I got sick and the school sent me home. I beeped Anthony and told him to meet me at Broadway Junction on the A train line. It was time that I spent QT with the man that I had fallen in love with before he had to leave me for a year. Anthony and I went shopping and to dinner. Afterward, we went to his house and made love. It was like the first time again. It was as if he had never made love before.

Nevertheless, it was the first time he had licked and ate my vagina. That was a new experience for me. For me, I didn't think he would ever do that being that he would never express his feelings to me. Anthony was the type that you were unsure about how he felt about you because he kept his feelings to himself or only spoke to his mother about you. Anyhow, Anthony ate it like it was lobster. He sucked it up in his mouth like melted butter running from the lobster. I don't know what it did for him but for me it brought me into some new life experience with this man. I could not stop moaning his name. He had me open. Then he stuck his penis inside of my hot dripping vagina and he put me to sleep.

It was about two hours after our session when I woke up. It was about 9:00 p.m. and I decided to stay over. I went out of the bedroom and into the living room where I knew his mother would be. I asked her if it would it be ok for me to stay over and she said okay. I then called my parents and I told them that I would be staying over Anthony's. My mother asked, "What did Anthony's mother say about it?" I explained that she was ok with it. My mother said, "Well tomorrow you have some explaining to do." I hung up the phone and went back in the room and my fine man was lying on the bed, buck naked. I took off my sweats and I jumped on my favorite pony and road him all night long. I knew it was going to be a long time without my pony so I needed to take advantage of it while it was still around. I didn't go to work the next day. I called in sick and I stayed in the bed with Anthony like we planned. Ms. Barbour went to take the boys to school while I cooked breakfast for us as well as Ms. Barbour when she returned. I finished cooking and Ms. Barbour walked in and said, "Would you like to come with me young lady?" I thought to myself "what did I do wrong?" I slowly followed her into her bedroom and she handed me a set of keys. She said," This is your set of keys to this home." My mouth dropped. She went on to say, "Close your mouth, something might fly inside." There was nothing I could say but thank you. Ms. Barbour said, "You know Anthony will be leaving so you may stay if you choose to at anytime." I was very grateful for her offer. I gave her a big kiss and a hug and then she asked, "Is my breakfast done?" I smiled and said yes. After leaving Ms. Barbour, I entered Anthony's room and he said "What took you so long bringing my food?" I said nothing and showed him the keys. He said, "What?" I said, "Well before I could bring the food to the room your mother asked me to go to her room and she handed me a set of house keys and said that I am welcomed anytime." Anthony just smiled and said that his mom really liked me. For the next two day, we spent the evenings together and did everything we could think of in his bedroom. Anthony also made time for his peoples and his business. It was now the day that Anthony had to turn himself in. I decided not to go. I just couldn't see him in cuffs. Not now, not ever, so I didn't go. Instead, I went to work and just waited for his mother to beep me when she got home.

Chapter III

Motherhood

It was now the beginning of me being alone. I'm without a man. The man that I had spent so much time with in the past year was now gone. I began to feel out of place but knew I had to deal with it. It was time to man up. I couldn't be no punk and had to deal with the situation. I reunited with my best friend Rosie by going over to her place to cry. She was my pillow. She's my sister and was everything I needed from the start.

Rosie always made me feel like I was in control of everything. She would always tell me that I was strong and that I could take on Tarzan if I had to. My friend really believed in me and I loved her for that. There wasn't anything that Rosie wouldn't do for me and likewise, there wasn't anything I wouldn't do for her. Rosie was my home girl! We were like two peas in a pod, Heckle and Jeckle, and you can't forget Salt 'N' Pepper.

We enjoyed the day together and we spent time enjoying Rosie's daughter Jhanee. She was getting big and started to talk. Well, actually she began to curse. She was just like her mother, with a nasty mouth. Wherever we went out, Jhanee would curse. She would swear at her doctors, teachers, church family, and everyone else she came into contact with. She didn't mean to curse intentionally; it was something she heard all the time so she would repeat it. The curses weren't harsh. They were more like damn it, hell, and ass.

On Thursday, I was home and it was the second week that Anthony had been sent to prison when I received my first phone call from him. I cried tears of joy. I said, "Hello Mister!" and he said, "Hello to you Miss! Where have you been?" I replied "At work." "And after work?" asked Anthony. "I would come home but get depressed so I go to

Rosie's house." He asked, "I thought that you would be there but I didn't call there because I wanted to make sure that you were there before I started calling her house." I said, "What do you mean by that?" Anthony said, "I have been calling your house for about four days so now I will know where to call if I call your house and you are not at home. I know where to catch you. Is that alright?"

"Yes Mr. Barbour!"

"How are you doing?" said Anthony.

"Not well, missing you," I said.

"How are you taking care of everything?"

"Well. Everything is ok. Your mother does not need anything."

"Have you been to see my mother?" he asked.

"No. It's been hard."

"What, you can't face the house without me?"

"You got it," I replied.

"Is my girl a punk?"

"No! But, maybe."

"It's time to be a woman. You know the one I met a year ago," Anthony said.

"What does that mean?" I asked.

"You always made your own decisions so don't stop now. Get your butt to Far Rockaway and see if my mother needs anything."

"Okay. You are right. I should not be scared to face my past."

"I will call you tomorrow at my house."

"Okay."

"See ya and be good."

It was morning and it was back to the old drawing board. The only difference was that my man was not there. "Program card and ID please." As I grabbed the student's information along came Spanish Elliot. "What up McEachin?" "What up?" I said. "Well, Dee said he been trying to call you for a couple of days" and I said, "Okay. Thanks but I spoke to him last night." He said, "Okay, just checking up."

Third period I was at my post in the cafeteria and patrolled the doorways to make sure students did not try to bring in any guns, scissors and any other dangerous weapons in order to harm fellow faculty, staff or students. I found myself to be more alert since Anthony's departure.

It was different today. After work, I wasn't going to my usual spot at Rosie's but Anthony's instead. I was ordered to go there to make sure everything was alright. I called Rosie and told her I would see her later and that I had to check up on Ms. Barbour. She asked, "What happened?" I assured her that there was nothing wrong but that Anthony called and asked me to check on his mother and Rosie was okay with that of course. It was time for me to face my responsibility to my man and his family. I was devoted to my man.

I put my key in the keyhole and slowly opened the door to an empty house. No one was home yet. It was about 5:30 p.m. The season was spring so it was understandable that people were out in the streets enjoying the longer days. Nevertheless, I decided to go to our bedroom where I started to think of all the good times I had in the room. I began to cry but they were happy tears mostly and some sad tears but they were all good. As I wiped the tears off my face and walked into the kitchen, the front door opened and it was my man's mother. "Hi, Fita! How long have you been here?" she asked. "Not long Ms. Barbour. Maybe about a half an hour or an hour," I replied. She said, "I was going to call you tomorrow because I need to go shopping. We could make it a day amongst us." I thought it would be a great idea so I agreed to pick her up on Saturday. Afterwards, I left but then I stopped and realized that Anthony said he was going to call me at his mother's house so I turned right back around and went upstairs. "What happed?" asked Ms. Barbour. I said, "I almost forgot that Anthony is going to call me here at 7:30 p.m." "Oh! Okay baby. I will be in my room if he needs to speak to me."

At 7:30 p.m. sharp, the phone rang and it was Anthony. "How was everything? Where is my mother?" he asked. I said, "Okay. She's in her room." He said, "Let me speak to my mother." I called out, "Mom, answer the phone" and I hung up. About a half hour past before I got to speak with Anthony again. He said that his mother told him that we were going shopping for food and she needed some clothes for the boys and some house goods. He told me to take out two thousand dollars from the money he gave me before he left and thought that that should be enough to cover what was needed and anything else for the month. We also discussed me going up for my first visit. It would be the first time I would be going to see him and my first time at a prison. This was also my first time dealing with someone that was in jail. I was scared to go but I knew that it would be wrong not to so I told him that I would be there the following day. Then he gave me his information.

My baby was in C-76 in RikersIsland. He told me to put $100.00 in his commissary (an account in his name so that he could get soap, deodorant, and make telephone calls). We missed each other so much and couldn't wait to see each other the following day. At about 8:30 p.m., I got off the call and walked past Ms. Barbour's room on my way out to head home and she said, "I will see you on Saturday!" and I agreed and said good night.

When I got home, I couldn't sleep. I was so anxious for the next day to come. Once it did, I was so excited yet I had to wait until after I got out of work to see my man. Tuesday, Thursday and Saturday were the days of the week Anthony could be visited so I went on Tuesday from 12:00 p.m. - 8:00 p.m. Visitors must enter before that time or there was no visit. The visit could only be an hour and there was no close contact allowed. Correction Officers were around to watch every move you made. You couldn't kiss or anything. It was horrible. I could barely touch him. I was floored by what I saw and was very angry. As a result, I started to cry. Looking at him in his beige uniform and unshaven face bothered me. It was an experience that I never ever imagined. The view was very hurtful.

We talked and he could do nothing but tell me that he was going to be alright. As I continued to cry, he said, "Baby stop. I'll be alright. It's only for eight months to a year." But that didn't make it better. We talked and talked and before you knew it, the hour was up. A Correction Officer came over to the table where Anthony and I were sitting and tapped it, letting us know that our visit was over. We got up and quickly snuck in a kiss and said our good-byes. He said, "I will call you tomorrow baby." As I was leaving, I noticed how the gates and doors slammed. It was so loud. It would scare any person. I couldn't imagine being in jail let alone Anthony being there alone. However, he seemed okay. I was more worried about him then he was for himself.

When I returned home, I cried all night just thinking of what he could be doing. For the rest of the week, I went to work and went home. On Friday, I went to Far Rockaway to Anthony's house because I had to go and withdraw money from the bank since his mom needed to go shopping and take care of her bills. When I arrived at the house, Ms. Barbour was ready to go. We were off on our journey. We first went to the bank and took out two thousand dollars from Dee's account and went food shopping. We later went on to buy the boys some clothes and then paid the light, telephone, cable bills as well as the rent. After everything was done, there was about three hundred dollars left so I told Ms. Barbour to keep it just in case she needed money during the week. She said, "Do you need any?" "No. I'm okay. I'm going home," I replied. She asked, "Do you want to stay?" I said, "No, maybe next week after I come back from seeing Anthony." She said, "Okay. Call me when you get home." I nodded yes and gave her a kiss on the cheek and left. As time went on, I found myself spending a lot if time in the Rockaways with Anthony's mother. That was something that my parents could not understand especially my mother. Mothers never understood. She couldn't understand her daughter spending more time with someone else's mother besides her own. But my parents didn't know about the money. Ms. Barbour was always asking me for the money, who was I to say she could not have her son's money.

It's been a month since Anthony had been locked up in prison when his mother called me and begged me to go over to her house. While preparing to go over to Anthony's, I explained to my mother that I would be going to see his mother and would be home the following day. My mother understood that time around since I finally told her that Anthony was in prison. What she didn't understand was the reason why Anthony left the money with me.

When arrived to Anthony's house, Ms. Barbour was in her kitchen with a strange look on her face. I noticed she wasn't alone. She was with a young lady who was holding a little boy on her lap. "Fita, this is Lisa, Anthony's son mother" said Ms. Barbour. I was shocked. The situation was unexpected. The last thing I thought would happen was me meeting Anthony's baby's moma' and his child.

I looked at the little boy with his light skin, bushy eyebrows, full lips, wide noise and green eyes. The baby was surly my man's son. He looked just like Anthony with the exception of having his mother's eyes. Lisa said, "His name is Devon." "Hi, Devon!" I said. He looked at me with the "who the heck is this lady" face.

Devon was three year's old and Anthony and I had been together for about two years. Lisa came towards me and handed me a letter. I grabbed it and looked down at the paper, noticing that it was notarized and had her and a witness's signature on it. The letter was a written agreement that Ms. Lisa L. would be giving Ms. Rafaela McEachin full guardianship over her son Devon from that day forward and forever. Ms. Barbour looked at me. I was shocked. My eyes were as big as a doorknob. The first thing that entered into my mind was how the heck was I going to explain this to my mother? Then how am I going to take him home? Followed by, how am I going to take care of him? Who is going to babysit Devon? What my parents think of Anthony? And what is going to happen to my career? So many things were running through my mind. Lastly, what kind of woman would give her son up to a stranger? She ain't know me. We weren't cool like that. My mind was racing. After reading the document aloud to me, Lisa left. Her departure seemed cold.

I was 24 years old and I was elected to be a mother. I never even thought about having a child. Although I dreamt of motherhood, I never planned to have a kid at that age. I looked at Ms. Barbour and I said, "What am I to do?" She was in just as much shock. I grabbed the filthy child and decided to bathe and feed him, and we both went to bed in Anthony's room. The next morning, before I opened my eyes I prayed that when I opened them, the bad dream would be over. Guess what, it wasn't. I opened my eyes and the little boy was snuggled underneath my arms and I cried and cried and cried some more. How could she!

This was a new beginning for me in life. I began to wonder if I loved Anthony, I had to love the entire package and all that he carried with him such as a child. Anyhow, I decided to examine my new son's eyes, nose and checked for cuts and bruises. I then realized that he was bleeding a bit from his nose. My next move was to go to the doctor. I got dressed and went into Ms. Barbour's room and explained that I found something wrong with the baby and needed to have him checked by a physician. In addition, I asked if it was okay for Devon to stay at her house until I told my parents. She said, "Of course."

That same morning, I waited until Anthony called before I woke Devon up. I began to cook breakfast when the phone rang. Ms. Barbour shouted, "Fita LL asshole is on the phone!" That was Ms. Barbour's nickname for Anthony when she was upset with him. I ran to the phone, picked it up and said "Mister, you know your son here?" He said, "I heard. My mother just told me what happened. Is Devon ok? I replied, "No. I need to take him to a doctor." Why did I say that? Anthony went on and on about, "What's wrong with my son? Is he okay? How he look?" I told him I was planning on taking Devon to the doctor. All Anthony was worried about was his son's health, and having him in the best clothes and buying him whatever else he needed. "Who's going to take care of him? Who's going to watch him? What are you going to tell you mother?" said Anthony.

Ms. Barbour was raising two boys of her own, Raymond and Teron. Anthony was the oldest of the three. Although Devon is her grandson, it seemed as if it would be a bit difficult for her to care for a small child. That was something I worried about as well as Anthony. Before hanging up with Anthony, he asked that I take Devon with me on my visit to the prison so that he could see him. Here I was, twenty-four. I had a good job and a younger man who was locked up with plenty of money, and he had a three year old baby that didn't know me or his father. I went in the bedroom and just cried until I got tired and went to sleep.

When morning hit, I woke up and bathed Devon. Following the bath, I decided to call my mother and told her that I was going home on Sunday. She wasn't too happy with me but she said okay. I then woke up Ms. Barbour and asked her to watch Devon while I went shopping in order to purchase him some clothes. When I got home, I immediately dressed Devon and took him to the doctor so that he could get checked out before we visited his dad. This time, Ms. Barbour would be attending the visit as well.

Off we went to Rikers Island Prison where my man was being kept before he was sentenced to hard time. Anthony was at C-76, which was located in a juvenile building. I must say, it was a wild facility. As the visitors walked along the hallway with a Correction Officer (CO), we were given a form to fill out and later given a locker number where we needed to place our belongings. Once we completed that tasks, we would return the form for review and if approved, another CO would be called "in the back" to bring out the prisoner for the visit.

It was very hot in the prison. The month was April and you know the weather in April is pretty fickle. One day is nice and warm but not warm enough to put on your air conditioner. But before you know it, it's cold again but by then your apartment complex turned off your heat for the spring and summer season so you end up freezing at night. That's how April was during this time. Nonetheless, I had Devon on my lap trying to keep him still and to avoid creating anymore heat. Ms. Barbour was standing on line. The place was crowded and we had to wait for about two hours before we were able to visit with Anthony. In Rikers Island, I felt like they did such things so that you could get frustrated and want to go home and never go back. It's like they wanted us to some how give up on our loved ones.

When Anthony arrived on the visiting floor, I began to feel sick. I could not bare to see him the way he was. A man that was always sharp with his appearance. Having a face that was always cleaned cut and hair always cut short. Now, he was in the beige jumpsuit again and had a full beard and mustache with an afro. His appearance still took me by surprise and I started to cry. Call me a cry baby but in the moment I saw my life flash in front of me like death was upon me. Although it was my second visit, this time seemed different. I was there with his child. If it were my choice, this wouldn't have been a site I would have wanted my child to see. As Anthony approached us, he kissed me and asked me to stop crying and told me that this would be all over soon. Then he kissed his mother and gave her a huge hug. That was his girl. Anthony may have not acted like it but he was really a momma's boy in his own way. After the huge hug, he looked and stared at Devon and a tear fell from his eye. He hadn't seen Devon in over a year. He checked his hands, nose and ears. He just kept on examining him before he embraced him and then he said, "Make sure you take care of my son." I just shook my head and agreed that would. The visit was very enjoyable. We were one big happy family. Anthony said, "Baby, it hurts you to see me this way so just take care of our son and don't come up here anymore. I will be home in about four months." I was a bit taken back by the remark but I was okay with it. By that time, the visit was over and Anthony kissed us goodbye.

It was spring 1988 and here I was raising a son without my parents even knowing. I was keeping a secret from my parents like when you're a child and you play with an invisible person. I was a young lady that never kept secrets from my parents but this was something I could not tell them otherwise I would have been banned from Anthony mother's house; that could not happen. My son Devon needed me and I was the only one he trusted. I spent more and more time over Ms. Barbour's house. Before I knew it, it was August and four months had past. All that time was spent in the Rockaways with Devon and my family still didn't know about the child. They didn't even seem to realize how much time I spent at Ms. Barbour's house. They didn't really bother me about it. I guess my parents were so wrapped up in their grandchildren for the summer. By this time, my brother James and wife Vicky had three children - Victoria Holly, James Jr. III, and Stephanie Rebecca. It didn't matter much to me since I knew I was doing the right thing by taking care of Devon. Besides, Ms. Michelle was very lonely without her oldest son around so my parents understood that and so did I.

September was creeping up and that's when the problems started. It was time to go back to work and my parents no longer had their grandchildren. It was back to school so my nieces and nephew went back home for the fall and my parents now expected to see me each night after work. This was the time when it got rough for me. I would get pulled from where I lived at the end of Brooklyn on Crescent St. to Far Rockaway in Queens. If you know NYC, you know that it seemed like going from one side of the world to the next. It was the grace of God that allowed me to be able to pull this off without my parents finding out that I was raising Anthony's son. My schedule for the next few months consisted of going to work from home, go to far Rockaway from work, stay at Ms. Barbour's for a few hours until I put Devon to sleep, and then returned home and rested in order to do the same thing all over the following day. I divided the weekends with my parents and Anthony's family. This plan worked for a few weeks but then all hell broke loose.

My parents were trying to figure out why I was stretching myself so thin for this boy. One night, I was in Far Rockaway speaking with Michelle. Ms. Barbour and I were on a first name basis now. I said, "Michelle, this is getting to be difficult for me because I still live with my parents and they don't know about Devon." She looked at me and said, "Baby girl, I was waiting until you got tired of playing mother to tell you that it was time you gave Devon back." Michelle placed her index finger on my mouth and said, "I love my grandson but it is time that you give Devon back his mother. She needs to take responsibility of her son. She chose to have him not you." I looked at Michelle's as tears rolled down my face and I said, "I can't." "Yes you can," she replied. "I don't really know Lisa nor do you so you don't know what she is going to do next. She might call the police and say that you kidnapped him so you need to give him back." I looked at Michelle and I said, "He has been filling my plate for about four months of my life. I guess you're right. I can't give him back so you call Lisa and do it." I picked up my sweater and left.

   At three o'clock in the morning my telephone rang. I answered the phone and it was Michelle. She was screaming that Devon would not go to sleep without me. I told her to put Devon on the phone. I said, "Devon go to sleep. Grandma will bring you to see me on my job tomorrow so I will see you in the morning. Okay?" He said, "Okay." "Devon, give grandma the phone." Then I spoke to Michelle for a little while and hung up the phone. The next morning, Michelle got up and called Devon's mother Lisa and told her that the summer was over and that she needed to pick up her son and deal with her responsibility.

Chapter IV

Doing Me

It was October and the leaves were falling off the trees. I had now gotten back into my normal routine. I went to work and after work I would go home, check in with my parents and then head to Rosie's house. Rosie was my witch. She was my nigga'. It didn't get no bigger than that but if it did she would be my bigga' nigga'. She was my best friend for life. We were friends that would die for one another. This bond went back since we were eight years old after meeting in public school. As the days went by and it got colder with the months, I started to fill my time back to my old ways. Rosie and I would hit the clubs. It was a long way from being a mom back in Far Rockaway. I was now distant from Michelle and the rest of Anthony's family. I was in my own little world now. My world was not bad. It was fun during my prime years of being twenty four in a big city like N.Y. Hey! How could you go wrong? I worked hard during the week and partied on the weekends. But I was still faithful to my man. I got on my visits and made sure I kept his commissary tight and his food stacked. What more could a man in prison want?

It was cold as hell now and the holidays were getting ready to role in when I started becoming interested in one of my fellow co-workers. His name was Gene. I felt a bit weird. I never was attracted to a working man but Gene was different. Gene was nice and polite, older, and understanding to my needs (not sexually). He was someone that I could talk to. He didn't know my man but knew he was in prison. Gene had a very nice smile and was about 5'7" with dark skin, very bowlegged and husky. He was twenty eight at the time, the oldest man I had ever dated. I thought to myself, here I am young, gifted, and Black with $65,000 that my man left me and he is in prison. I am in the big city without him, what was happening to me? The strong young lady that he left in charge to take care of his money and family was about to fall for another man. How could Anthony leave me here? I began getting a bit angry and saddened by my situation with Anthony. I was a young light skinned sista', built like a brick house, full D cup breast, small waist, big video booty, and some hips that men would die for. How could he leave me and think that my desires would not one day roar?

It was now the holidays and I was going to my family's house to spend time with them for the holidays. But this year, after I ate, I made my way to the Rockaways to spend some time with my man's family. I hadn't seen Michelle in about four months but would speak with her and sent her money from Anthony's account. Nonetheless, my car was in the shop for the holidays which sucked so I took the train instead. I hopped on the J train to Broadway Junction and transferred to the A train to Far Rockaway and got off on Beach 98 St. Anthony's family lived in Bay Towers. Michelle hooked up a good dinner. She was a very good cook just like my family. She cooked a lot of the same dinner items as my family minus the Spanish dishes. That was my mother's department of course. My mom Hilda was straight from Puerto Rico so no one could touch her meals. But my father James was African American and he cooked soul food. I must admit that I was very blessed because I still had both my parents and in my days many parents were not together. My friends and even my man didn't have two parents in their lives so I consider myself lucky and special. Dinner was great. It was time for me to go home. I kissed everyone goodbye and told Michelle that I would try and keep in better touch with her and she agreed to the same.

A week after Thanksgiving, I began to see more of Gene. We spoke on a daily basis in addition to working together. But we never shared the same post except at the cafeteria where all units were assigned to at certain times of the day. By the second week of December, Gene had asked to take me out on a date and I agreed. We decided on dinner at a small Chinese restaurant named *Kum Kow* that was on Mertle and Washington Ave in Clinton Hill. The restaurant had some of the best Chinese food around. People from all over the city would flock to BK to get food from *Kum Kow's*. At the time, it was a take out place and it had about four small tables for customers to sit at. The place wasn't fancy but it was to me and Gene, at least for that night. We decided to sit and talk. We spoke about life and he told me about his separation from his wife and that he had three children, two boys and one girl. His oldest son was not from his wife, he was from a previous relationship. Then Gene switched up the conversation to talk about things like seeing each other on a regular basis. I was not sure of what to say. At the same time, I was feeling like I really liked Gene and I didn't want to lose out on some enjoyment in my life so I told him that, "For the record, you do know that this could not get serious. I have a man and he will be coming home in a few months. When that time comes, this will have to end…" Gene said he was just fine with that. He agreed that the relationship we had would be platonic.

"Merry Christmas!" said Gene with a big box wrapped in red satin material just for me. It was December 26, 1988 when I saw Gene again. I had spent the holidays with my family and Anthony's family. I was shocked by the nice gesture and did not expect anything from him. It had only been a few weeks since we had been seeing each other. I cried because the gift came as a total shock to me. I'm very sentimental and didn't know how else to react. He ordered me to open the gift and as I started un-wrapping the box, I began to reminisce on unwrapping the first gift Anthony had given me. It was a Gucci chain with a charm of Jesus Christ with rubies and diamonds. Gene's gift was just as nice. It was a black leather trench coat with a black mink collar. I thanked him and I cried with joy. But in the back of my mind I couldn't stop thinking about the fact that I didn't buy him anything. I began to feel bad so I left feeling like I owed him something. During that time in my life, I felt that I had to repay a man for gifts that were given to me. Therefore, the next morning I got up and went shopping to buy him a gift. I returned with a gold chain covered with diamonds. After I gave him the gift, it was a rap. We started spending a lot more time together.

Gene introduced me to his mother and sister Debra. She and I were the same age so we hung out from time to time. He also introduced me to his children Tanginia, Tarell, and Robert, who was the oldest. We were like a family when we went out. Spending a few days with Gene's family had resulted in me not speaking with Rosie. As soon as I realized I hadn't called her, I rushed to the phone to let her know that I would be stopping by her house to give her a Christmas gift and to gossip. When I arrived to Rosie's house, we immediately exchanged gifts. I had bought her a pair of earrings and she bought me a ring. We were both excited to flaunt our new jewelry with all of the other items we had given each other throughout the year. We always bought each other stuff. It was something Rosie and I always did. She was the sister I never had. Anyhow, we got to talking and I told Rosie that I was very happy with Gene. She quickly reminded me that I didn't have much time to be happy with him because Anthony would be arriving home soon. But she turned around and told me to enjoy it anyway because I deserved it. She said, "Don't forget you can't get serious. It's too close to Anthony's return now and besides how are you going to explain all the money you

and his mother spent?" I replied, "Please....I got this!" and I went home.
    Of course my parents liked Gene but didn't like all that came with him. You know, his package – three kids and two baby mamas. Nevertheless, my mother from time to time would also remind me of my man Anthony and I would say, "Mom, he is away. I will be fine when he comes home." I would say this for months. Next thing I knew it, it was January and I had been involved with Gene for quite sometime. I was now cool with his family. And YES, I had been intimate with him. It was New Years Eve when I finally decided to have sex with him. It wasn't exactly the way I had planned to spend the New Year. I really wanted to be with the man that I loved but he was away in prison and there was nothing I could do about it. Although I wasn't in love, Gene was special and we spent a lot of time together and with his children. We went to the movies and ate out at nice restaurants. We spent a lot of money on each other – his, mine, and money I had been "awarded." Gene was there during the times I needed someone most; those were the times I needed someone to hold me, touch me and comfort me. As time went on, I got to know the "real Gene." It's true when someone tells you that "you don't know a man until you live with him." Well I experienced that first hand.
    We had decided to get a room together on Monroe St. between Nostrand and Bedford. It started out as a place where we could get down and dirty in (if you know what I mean). We were two consenting adults, but I still lived with my parents and he had his kids. Nevertheless, during this short period, I began seeing things I didn't like and did not want to live with. Gene had a drinking problem. In addition, he would have mood swings, an attitude, and would show constant aggression. His loud voice while under the influence was upsetting to me plus he wouldn't remember anything the next day. I could not take it anymore. After about three months, I had to break away. I must admit, it was a bit difficult because I knew he was a nice guy and had problems but they couldn't become my problems. During the time of my breakaway, I had not realized that it was the month of March and it was Anthony's month of release. I hadn't remembered because I was so wrapped up in my relationship with Gene. I recall talking to Rosie the evening of March 10, 1989 and had explained to her how I was thinking about breaking up with Gene. She said, "Well you need to do something because Anthony will be home next week...I have been calling you and you have not returned my calls. Because I have been trying to remind you that it is March and you know that Anthony will be home on the 17th so Ms. Fita Flame you need to do something not now but right now!" I hung up the telephone feeling anxious. What was I going to do? How am I

going to explain the money? What if he found out that I had someone in my life? There were so many things racing in my head that it made me confused.

The next morning, I woke up and decided to go talk to Gene and tell him that it was time for us to go our separate ways. He could not understand. But I explained to him that I could not deal with his drinking and just needed to be by myself. Gene apologized and he said he understood. Therefore, that duty was done; at least that's what I thought. When I went to the room that Gene and I shared, I started to gather my things to take them back home. Home for me was Crescent St. between Atlantic and Fulton with my parents. When I got home, I put my things down and went to Rosie's house. Finally, it was back to normal. We were just kickin' it, when of course she had to ask how was the sex. I replied, "Okay." She said, "Girl, it was more than ok." "Well, it was good but not good enough to take me from my man." Anthony got what it takes for a woman stay home. Rosie said, "I guess you are leaving a man that you spent five months with, lived with, and had taken care of you in all ways and now you are back home." She was right but it was only fun while it lasted (that was the last of that conversation).

Rosie and I decided to go shopping. That was our hobby, like every other woman in this world. The next morning, I went to work. This was the first morning after my breakup with Gene. I almost forgot we still worked together. I saw him and he looked sad. His face was grim. It kinda' looked like he had lost his best friend or something. I said good morning to everyone and went on with my daily procedures. However, at about noon Gene said, "I need to talk to you." I agreed to speak with him but it needed to be at the end of the day and he said, "Fine." After work, Gene and I decided to go out to eat to talk about whatever he wanted to talk about. We ended up at a fish and chip joint on Willoughby and Bridge St. It was a Chinese place that was one block from where we worked. I was still at Westinghouse H.S. Gene talked about how he needed me and I explained to him that I needed some time to myself. He had no idea that it was time for Anthony to arrive home and I didn't mention it. Besides, I needed to leave my opportunities open. "Never leave a poor rat with one hole to grow in." I didn't want to be the poor rat if Anthony were to mess up. The rest of the week, I went home and engaged in my daily routine - I went to work and went home and spent a lot of time with my parents and my friend Rosie. I couldn't fool my parents. My mother and father knew what I was doing. But I was trying to avoid discussing what I had been involved in for the past eight months. My parents were just glad that I had left Gene alone. At 25 years old, my parents were proud at the fact that I was not a statistic –

a young woman with a child, no education, and strung-out on drugs. Growing up in the hood did impact many people around me. Brooklyn was no joke. My parents knew that they had done a fine job. I was a first generation college student, so I definitely knew that I was blessed. Not many people in my family or neighborhood went to college.

On March 15, 1989, two days before my big debut with my man Anthony who was coming home, I began to get nervous. Rosie was no help; she kept me more nervous than ever. I had told Rosie that Gene wanted to see me. Rosie swore she knew me so well and that I would go, but just to prove her wrong I didn't go. By Friday, March 16, 1989, my beeper went off while at work and it was Michelle. "When you get off of work you gotta' go to the bank and get your man five thousand dollars. He needs to go to the barber shop and shopping," said Michelle. I replied, "Okay." After work, I went to the bank to withdraw the money and then headed to Rosie's house; that was a bad idea. Rosie and I ended up going to *Celebrity* where I got drunk and ended up in Gene's bed on Monroe St. What a bad move.

Saturday, March 17, 1989, I jumped up and Gene said, "What's wrong?" I said, "I got to go! I have something to do at Rosie's house." Gene had no idea that Anthony was getting out that day. I called my house and my mother said that Ms. Michelle called looking for me. My mom asked, "Where were you last night?" I said, "I was in Rosie's house." Just when I said mommy, with a questionable voice, my mom said, "I know you won't be home until Sunday." I said, "Thank you for understanding." My father got on the phone to tell me he loved me. They knew Anthony was getting out on the 17th and that I would be spending time with him and his family. I called Rosie and I asked, "What the hell happened last night?" "You got so drunk and wanted to go home! You know I don't drive. Your beeper kept going off so I answered it and it was Gene so I asked him to take you home. I told him you were at the club drunk so he said okay. I had no idea that he was taking you to Monroe St. I thought he was taking to Crescent." I said, "Okay witch, whatever! I'm coming over there to take a shower and I got to go to Far Rock."

"Pimpin' ain't easy!" I got to Rosie's house and had to move fast. Anthony was getting home at 12:00 p.m. and it was now 9:30 a.m. I got in the shower and I put on my Calvin Klein mini jean dress and navy blue stockings with my black Calvin Klein boots that zipped up my calves. I put my hair up in a bun and grabbed my black coach bag and left. I jumped into my rental and went to Far Rock. It was now 11:00 a.m. and I was on the Belt Parkway in a traffic jam. I was beginning to get nervous and anxious. I couldn't, for the life of me, remember if there was another way to get to Far Rock from where I was. In NYC traffic, you could think of a lot of things! I was trying to figure out how I was going to explain the money situation. It was $45,000 missing. After Friday's withdrawal, there was only $15,000 left.

Chapter V

Home Coming

It was noon and I was still trying to get to Bay Towers to Anthony's house for his home coming. My beeper was beeping and it read, "911. 911." I kept driving because back in the day I didn't have a cellar phone to use. It was nothing I could do. I knew that when my beeper went off that meant that he was at his house already. After exiting the bridge, it would take me about 10 minutes to get to his house. My stomach started to cramp. I wasn't sure what that meant. Was I getting my period? Or was I nervous?

When I walked in the house, everything got quiet. Everyone was looking at me with weird faces. I said, "What's wrong Ms. Michelle?" She said, "He left. He went to the barber shop for his hair cut. You know your man." I thought to myself, "Dang! He couldn't wait?" I asked to speak to Ms. Michelle privately in her bedroom and she agreed. I asked," What do you plan to tell him about the money that is not accounted for?" She said, "Fita, I'm his mother." And that's all she said. I said to myself, "I guess I'm going to have to explain the money!" We both got up and left her room. I decided to take a nap in Anthony's bed while I waited for him to return home.

At 4:00 p.m., I woke up and everyone was there except Anthony. His cousin Dinkie, some people from the building, and other random guest. Everyone was eating and celebrating Anthony's dismissal from prison. By 6:30 p.m., people began to get restless, wondering where the heck Anthony was. Minutes later the door bell rang and I began to get nervous but ready for my man. When Ms. Michelle opened the door it was Anthony and he looked good. I could have eaten him up alive. In came Anthony and then Becky. "What the hell?" The trick that Anthony was dealing with before we got together. My mouth dropped to the floor. I was about to kick him in his own house. I said, "Anthony, come to the room." He said, "Okay. Wait one minute." When we got to the room I said angrily, "You Stupid! What is wrong with you? " He replied, "She's just a friend." I asked, "Oh! So is that why you didn't need anything while you were away?" And he blatantly replied, "Yeah!" "Anthony, so what does that mean?"

"Nothing. She is my girl, " he said.

"What am I?"

"Baby, you are my woman"

"What does that mean in you

world?" I asked.

"Baby, you are marriage material and mother material. She was just my girl."

Anthony sounded so stupid to me that I said my goodbyes to everyone and left. I was pissed, not realizing what I had done to him. I wasn't that faithful myself. Nevertheless, I was very hurt and embarrassed because this situation happened in front of all of his family and friends. When I left, I decided to go to Rosie's house to cry my head off and to explain to her what had happen to me. I walked into Rosie's house with my bulging red eyes and she asked, "What happened? Did Anthony argue about the money that is missing?"

I looked at Rosie and said, "No."

"So why are you here? And why are you crying?"

"He had the nerve to come in the house with Rebecca," I said.

"You are not talking about Becky his ex-girl?"

"Yes!"

"What is up with that witch?" asked Rosie.

"I don't know but I did not tell him about the money either? I just argued with him about Becky and then I left."

Rosie asked, "So what up? Did you ask him about her?"

"Yeah! He gave me some sob answer like I was marriage material and mother material and that Becky was his girl. Whatever that meant."

So while I was crying my eyes out at Rosie's house, Anthony and his crew were having a good ol' time at his place. Rosie said to me, "So that is why you had a good time when he was away. Days like this, you should just reflect on the good times you had with Gene."

I replied, "You are right." I didn't go home that night. I didn't want my parents to know that things backfired on me, so I just stayed at Rosie's house that entire weekend and never told my parents. On Sunday, I got up early and went home.

When I got home, my mother asked, "How is Anthony?" I

said, "He fine. Thanks for asking mommy." She then asked, "Is there something wrong?" I instantly said, "No. Why?" My mother said, "There is something you need to know Rafaela. That is that I gave you life and I could always tell when something is wrong. You might fool your father but not me my child." I began to cry and explained to my mom what had occurred at Anthony's house. My mother said, "Baby, everything in life is not as easy as you would want it to be." "What do you mean?" I asked. "Whatever you do in life will always reflect on you for the days to come," said my mom. "What is that suppose to mean?" "Fita, you aren't stupid so don't act like you don't know what I'm saying. If you want me to break it down in your street terms then I will. I'm saying that what you did in the months that Anthony was away, to you it might have been a slick move, but in God's eyes it was not cool and he gave you a task that you didn't pass so for that you will have to pay." I said, "So God wants me to hurt?" "No but by you accepting the money that Anthony left behind willingly meant you would have to do right by God and not by Anthony. For that is why you will have a few troubles to come. "Mommy, so now what?" "I can't fix it. It's up to you to fix it. You are a young lady and very smart. You think about what I have said and fix it."

I went in my room and I thought about the last few months of my life and the role that I played. I asked God to forgive me. I then understood that my mother was saying that if I was not going to be faithful to Anthony that I should not have accepted the money. It was dinner time and I sat at the table with my parents. My father said, "Hey baby girl! How was you weekend?" I said, "Good daddy."

He asked, "How is Anthony?"

"He's good daddy."

"Tell him I said hello and to stay home."

My daddy was very cool. I was daddy's girl. Whatever I wanted, my daddy would give to me. My brother was a momma's boy. Anything that Junior wanted, mommy gave him. Nonetheless, our family was a tight knit. The next morning, was back to the old drawing board for me. Back to work from 8:30 a.m. to 4:30 p.m. each day, Monday thru Friday. Regardless of my complaints, I was still committed to my job. I never missed work unless I was very sick. I needed to be halfway dead before I called out sick. I did this for two weeks before Anthony called me to go over to his house. I just figured it would be for his money so I was prepared to tell him what happened.

When my beeper first went off, I looked and noticed it was Anthony's number. I was busy at work and called when I got some free time. While on my lunch break, I called Anthony. When he picked up the phone, he said, "Wow! You stayed away for over a week and didn't come see your man?" I said, "Well my man was so busy with his girl that he could not call his woman."

"You really need to quit it. If Becky meant something to me I would have left her the money."

"True that... Well, I'll be over there on the weekend."

"Okay! Will I get to spend some quality time with my woman?" said Anthony.

"Yes, of course."

I knew that that meant we were going to make love; some passionate love, the love that I had been missing for eight months. The kind of love only Anthony could give me.

By Friday, I was anxious. After a long day of work, I went home to an empty house. My parents weren't home from work yet. In the meantime, I gathered some clothes and I wrote a note to my parents letting them know that I would be at Anthony's house so to call me there if they needed to speak to me. When I arrived to Anthony's, I knocked on the door. He shouted, "When did you start knocking on the door? Don't you have a key?" I laughed and put my key in the door. As I slowly opened the door, I noticed Anthony was standing directly on the other side of the entrance with his Nautica jeans, minus a shirt. His ripped, clean cut body was so man-ish and sexy to me. His horny butt picked me up and dropped me on his bed and had his way with me. I had no complaints. He started to undress me while kissing me all over my body. First my breast and then he worked his way down. Meanwhile, he unbuckled my pants and slid them right off my body. By this time, I was so hot and horny that I just wanted him to stick his thick stick half up inside of me and took me to his world; the world that I had missed for eight months. Anthony and I made love all night until we both fell asleep.

On Saturday morning, I got up from the bed and took a shower and before I could turn around there was the big boy in the shower with me, touching my body passionately. Anthony's way of starting an episode in the shower was by touching my butt and then off to sucking my nipples. Next he began to play with my vagina by placing his finger inside of me, getting me wetter than water itself. His touch caused me moan, "Aye poppy!" and I called out his name. At last, he stuck his penis inside of me and I was in heaven. After love making in the shower, he washed my body and I washed his and then we exited the shower to start our day.

My day was cut out for me. Mr. Man planned on us going shopping. We started out by going to breakfast at IHOP in Five Town's

Plaza. Then he wanted to go to a Toyota dealer. I knew that we were going shopping but I did not know that it would be for a car. When we got to the dealership, Anthony had his heart set on a 1989 Hunter Green Four-Runner Truck. A sales person approached us and said, "Good Afternoon! I see you're interested in the truck." "Yes. What's the price on the Four-Runner?" asked Anthony. "It's $25,500," said the sales person. Anthony asked, "You like mommy?" "Yes poppy," I replied. Anthony then took $10,000 out of his pocket and handed it to the sales person and told the guy he will be back next week for his truck. In 1989, there weren't many people into trucks like people are now. This was a big thing for Anthony and me.

Following our time at the dealership, it was on to my favorite part of the day and that was shopping for clothes and shoes. That's what girls do best, besides shopping for household items. While shopping for clothes, I began to find it strange that Anthony hadn't brought up the issue of the money to me yet. Anyhow, after shopping for clothes and shoes, we began to wrap-up our evening with dinner at Red Lobster. During dinner, I decided that I was going to bring up the topic of the money, just so I could get if off of my chest. "Poppy, why have you not asked me for your money yet?" I asked. Anthony said, "Cause' I know that my woman is trustworthy and I know that it's plenty of money in the account that I left before I went away." I said, "Well, when you want it, it will be there for you" and I left it at that and I continued to eat my lobster.

Our day was beautiful. I didn't want it to end. It was 10:00 p.m. when we got to Anthony's and I heard Ms. Michelle say, "Fita!" "Yeah Ms. Michelle?" I said. "I'm glad that you two fixed your differences," said Ms. Michelle.

"Yes we have. Thanks!"

"Don't thank me. The boy is in love. He just doesn't know how to admit it. Before you go in the room, I need to speak to you Fita."

"Okay Ms. Michelle," I said.

Anthony was just laughing and smiling. "What's so funny?" I asked. "That I just don't understand how my mother likes you so much. She has never been like this with any other girl that I have ever had." "That's because I'm not your girl. I'm your woman. You made that clear to me," I replied. Anthony then left the living room and went to his bedroom. "I'm going to talk to your mother and then I will be in the room." Anthony said, "Mommy, don't be long. Poppy got a surprise for you ok?" I smiled and said, "Yes."

I walked in Ms. Michelle's bedroom and I said, "You wanted to talk to me?" Ms. Michelle said, "Fita, do you love my son?" I said,

"Yes." "You know that you are a few years older than my son and he is still a young man and he just doesn't know what to do with a woman like you so if you love this man you will have to deal with the steps of him maturing."

I said, "Yes…"

"Well, you need to know that he doesn't know how to tell you that he loves you but he told me last night in a conversation."

"Thank you Ms. Michelle," I replied.

"It's our secret."

As I walked into the bedroom, Anthony was buck-naked, pretending to be asleep. I took my clothes off to lay next to him and Anthony turned around and got on top off me. He asked, "Is everything alright?" "Yes," I replied. "So you were going to sleep?" I said, "No. I was just waiting to see how long before you jumped on me." Anthony laughed and said, "You know that I can't resist you in the bed buck-naked." I said, "Well…" (like Al Green). At that point, Anthony put his hand on my naked body playing with my breast and then moved down to my belly button and started to lick it very sensually. I began to moan the words poppy as he stuck his magic stick inside of me. We made love all night, just like the night before, and then went to sleep.

Sunday was family day, so I got up and showered, and went to my house. I left Anthony sleeping. When I got home, my parents were sleep as well. I decided to go to my room and go back to bed. I woke up around 4:00 p.m. to my mother cooking dinner. It smelled so good. The aroma of arroz con habichuelas (rice and beans) and pernil (roast pork) filled the air. My mother said, "You came home and went to sleep?" I said, "Yes mommy. We did so many things this weekend that I did not sleep much." "Well it's time to come and eat and then get yourself together for tomorrow," she said. "Okay," I replied.

Monday morning, I was in my glory. The weekend went so well that I couldn't stop smiling. Me and my man chilled and we discussed a lot of things that we needed to get in order. After work, I went to my girl Rosie's. She was like my bible. We talked about my weekend with Anthony and Rosie said, "That boy love you and you know that." I said, "Yes. I know." I didn't go much into detail about our weekend. One thing that I was taught was never to discuss love making with your man to anyone; not even with your best friend. Therefore, we never discussed my sex life. Rosie was my girl and we discussed everyone else's sex life or any other guy we had been with but our main men was out of the question. That was our rule. Rosie said, "So did you discuss the money?" I said, "Not really. You know Anthony, he doesn't need it yet so I did not mention it." "You are crazy!" "Rosie, what am I suppose to do? Just say I spent up your money? "

Rosie said, "I don't know. You should try to get that out of the way though. "

"Girl, in time I will."

"Yeah right! So what did you get when you went shopping?"

I told her that Anthony bought me two pairs of Calvin Klein Jeans, two Benetton Shirts, a Nautica Goose Jacket, a pair of sneakers, brown boots, and some jewelry.

"I got to talk to you later. I have to call Anthony."

"Okay. Talk to you later," said Rosie.

As time went on, I started staying more and more at Anthony's house. It was like we were living together. I was going to work from his house and going to my home afterward. It had been six months later and I was at my house when I called Anthony and Ms. Michelle answered the telephone. "Mom?" I said. "Fita?" said Ms. Michelle.

"Yes."

"I thought you were in the room?"

"No. It's not me."

By this point Ms. Michelle was upset. She yelled, "Boy you betta' come get this phone

"Who is it?" asked Anthony.

Ms. Michelle said, "PICK UP THE PHONE!"

I heard Anthony say wait to someone in the room with him. When he picked up the phone, I said "Hey! What up?" Anthony acted as if things were cool and replied, "Nothing. Just getting some rest."

I said, "Anthony who is there with you."

"No one."

I said, "You're lying. I heard a voice."

"You are hearing things."

"You want to start lying?"

"You are bugging," he said and hung up the phone.

I immediately called back. When he picked up the phone, I said, "You hung up on me. Who are you trying to impress?" Anthony said, "I'M BUSY!" and hung up again. I was hurt. At this time, I wanted to go over there to find out who was in my bed.

I called back again and a girl answered the telephone.

I asked, "Where's Anthony?"

The girl said, "He doesn't want to talk to you Fita."

I said, "Who is this?"

The girl said, "It's Becky."

"Becky you tell Anthony that this is it! I never want to see him again. Tell him don't come to my house or to my job."

"He won't," said Becky.

"GO TO HELL," I said and hung up.

It was happening again. This stupid slut was getting in the way of me and Anthony. I was so mad that I screamed and my parents jumped up frightened thinking something had happened to me and yelled, "What's wrong?" I said, "Nothing, just something that Rosie told me...Mommy and daddy, I'm going to Rosie's house." "Okay, just call when you get there," said my mom.

"I will hurt him Rosie!" I said storming through Rosie's front door. "What are you talking about?" said Rosie. "I called Anthony's house and his mother answered the phone and she said she thought I was in the room..." Rosie looked at me and saw the devil in my eyes. Before I could finish my sentence, she said, "Look, why don't you just calm down. I want you to breathe and then we will talk." "But Rosie," I said. "It doesn't have to be a girl in the room." I looked at Rosie and said, "If his mother thought that I was in the room then that meant that she heard a woman's voice. Rosie but you need to hear the rest of the story." Rosie said, "My ears are open." "I spoke to him and he tried to act like he was asleep and then he hung up. I called back and Ms. Becky answered the telephone!" Rosie looked at me and she just opened her arms and knew that I was going to cry. She said, "I know that you love him but I don't know what his intensions are. I love you Fita. You are my best friend and you need better in your life." I said, "Thank you for the love that you give to me. Promise me that we will keep loving each other regardless of our decisions of love." Rosie said, "We were two little girls in school and we are two big girls just learning to live so I will never leave you. We are friend forever. I think that you should just leave him alone until you get yourself together. You are going to make yourself sick with his bull. I'm your friend and I don't want to see you crazy over him. It's not worth it. You are beautiful so don't let this be the end of your beauty." I looked at Rosie and said, "Thank you!" I began to feel much calmer. Her words soothed me. Rosie was like my counselor. She was someone that I would take advice from; you know a girl always has her friend that gives her advice like "Dear Abby."

I began to ponder, where was Becky when he went to jail? Where was Becky when Devon needed to be taken care of? Why didn't he leave her the money? Why did I have to go through this? I returned home that night. Before I got into my house, I had to get myself together before my parents noticed something was wrong with me. My mother was good at sensing this kind of thing. There she goes, "Is everything alright?" my mother asked. "Yes mommy. Rosie and her boyfriend were going through some things." "Oh! Okay," she replied.

The next day, my pager went off while I was at my post at the front door asking the students for identification to get into the building. When I looked down, it was Anthony paging me so I ignored it. It vibrated again, and again, and I continued to ignore it. At 2:00 p.m., it went off again. This time, it was his mother calling but I decided to ignore it once more. Before I got off of work, my beeper went off again and it was my mother. This time I answered. My mother asked if I was going directly home after work. I assured her that I would be. She asked if I could cook dinner and I said yes.

When I got home, I began to cook and the phone rang. I noticed on the caller ID that it was Anthony calling so I didn't answer. This went on for two weeks. In the meantime, I continued to live my life ignoring him. By the weekend, Rosie was calling telling me how Anthony had called her on Friday. Rosie asked me if I knew that Anthony was trying to reach me for about two weeks. I said, "Yes but I was ignoring his calls." Rosie asked if I noticed that Anthony's mother was trying to call me. I explained to her that I did see them but also ignored them thinking she was calling me for Anthony. Rosie then asked me to go over her house since she needed to talk to me and I agreed. By 3:00 p.m., I was getting ready to go to Rosie's house when the telephone rang. It was Anthony. He first spoke to my father and then my father handed me the phone telling me that it was important.

I said, "Hello!"

Anthony said, "Hi! How are you?"

"Fine," I replied.

"I didn't ask you how you look. I asked you how do you feel."

"I don't have time to play games," I said.

"I need to talk to you."

"Okay but it will have to be tomorrow."

Anthony asked, "Why not tonight?"

"I can't. I have a dinner date."

Anthony was shocked. He said, "WITH WHO?" "None of your business. Your business is Becky remember?" I said. Anthony said, "Okay. Well tell him that he better be careful." I just laughed and I hung up. Later that evening, I went to Rosie's house. I was wondering what she wanted to talk to me about. "What is up?" I said. "You know that Anthony is messed up right now so he is going to ask for his money tonight?" she said. I said, "Okay, but I'm not meeting him tonight."

"You not?"

"I said no!"

She said, "So did you speak to him?"

"Yes. I told him that it will be tomorrow."

"Did he agree?"

"Yes."

Rosie said, "What could Anthony do? He know he was caught dead wrong. He knows that you're finally serious." I said, "Yes!" Rosie asked me where was I going dressed all nice. "I have a date," I said. "With who?" "Gene..." Rosie's eyes got as big as a crack-head. Rosie said, "Well when did this episode begin?" "It's been a week" Rosie said, "Be careful," then I left.

That night was full of laughter. Gene knew what to say when he wanted my attention and we just enjoyed the night. It was 12:00 a.m. when my beeper went off. It was Anthony and I stopped at a phone booth to call him back. "Yeah, what up?" He asked, "Are you home so I could come and get you?" I said with an attitude, "No Anthony!" He asked, "What the hell you doing?"

"I don't think that's any of your business."

"Don't let me hurt you."

"This is not Becky you are talking to," I said.

"I don't care about Becky."

"You don't care much about me either," I said.

At that point, Gene was listening in on the conversation. He asked, "Are you alright?" I responded, "Yes" and went back to my conversation with Anthony. Anthony said, "Who the hell is that? And where are you at twelve o'clock at night?" "Anthony, I'm still out with a friend of mine. It's not your business where I'm at." Anthony was now frustrated and was threatening me saying that I better be home in one hour because he was going to get me. I just laughed and hung up. I knew that I had Anthony in the palm of my hand now. I had his money so I had the power. But what Anthony didn't know was that I did not have all his money.

It was 3:00 a.m. and I had just opened the door. There was a note from Anthony on the floor. He must have stuck it under the door and it read:

I was here and you were not home.
I will pick you up at 10:00 a.m. so be prepared.

I thought to myself, here goes my Sunday morning in an argument. I took a shower and went to sleep. I woke up at 7:00 a.m., showered again, and started preparing myself (being that Anthony and I have not seen each other in one month). I had to make sure I looked extra good. I wore my tight Moschino jean jumpsuit that had a bottle flare, my square toe black Gucci boots with my black leather trench that had a mink collar (the one Gene bought me) and my hair was in Shirley temple braids. I put on my jewels that Anthony bought me, the Gucci chain with the Jesus Christ medallion that was covered with diamonds and rubies. Lastly, I placed my diamond earrings on my ears and stuffed my Gucci bag with all my personal items. I was sharp and very impressing.

I decided to go over to Anthony's house so that my parents would not know that we were at war. Ten o'clock on the nose the telephone rang and it was Anthony. I answered the phone and I said I'm coming down. I wrote a note for my parents, letting them know that I went to Anthony's and to call me if they needed something. When I got downstairs, Anthony had a face of death. He looked furious. If looks could kill, I would have been dead. I said, "Good Morning!" Anthony asked, "What's good about the morning?" I sarcastically said, "You are with me and you're alive." Anthony asked me how my dinner date was and I said it went real good. "You must have done more than just eat up to three in the morning." I said, "Let's not go there." Anthony looked at me and said "What the hell is wrong with you?"

"What do you mean?"

I said, "No, he's just a friend."

He looked at me and shook his head, "So you got another man?"

"So you deserved that."

"What do I deserve Anthony; I don't deserve you in and out of my life. When we get to your house, I'm going to give you all your money and I will take the train home," I said.

"Who is he?" Anthony asked.

"He is nice and he respects me, and I have no drama."

The next time Anthony opened his mouth, he said, "But he has three kids and a wife. That's more drama then you could handle and you know it." I was shocked that he knew all of that information. I was speechless. I just stood there in deep thought trying to figure out how the hell he knew all that info. Who was his informant? Who was watching me? Who was keeping tabs on me? How much did he know? Did he know that I was messing with him while he was away? How long did Anthony know about him? Anthony said, "Yeah Gene; the School Safety Officer." My heart fell to the ground. At this time, I knew that I was going to die. Anthony was going to kill me at his mother's house. I had to call Rosie. She was the only one that knew all that information but Rosie was my girl. I just started tripping about the situation. It had to be someone that Anthony knew, not my best friend.

I asked Anthony if his mother was home and he said yes. I asked him about her plans for the day and he wasn't sure. As we got into the parking lot of Bay Towers, I started to get nervous and scared. I looked up at the window and Ms. Michelle was looking out of the window. I felt relieved and I knew that he was not going to kill me in front of his mother. As we got on the elevator, I looked at Anthony and he was pissed. I put my key in the door and Ms. Michelle greeted me with a smile. Ms. Michelle said, "What's wrong Fita? The both of you need to get your act right." I just smiled and went to the room. As I closed the door behind me, Anthony asked if I spent his money on Gene.

"What?" I replied.

Anthony said, "You hear me."

"No. I have money of my own."

"Is there anything you want to clear up?" he asked.

"No! Let's just get to the point."

Anthony said, "I'm a little messed up with the business and I need you to withdraw some money."

"I will but it all back in your name."

"So that means that you are not going to be a part of me?"

I said, "That's correct."

"Okay. I will take you to the bank tomorrow."

"Okay but there's something you need to know and you may be very upset but I can't keep living this way. So I will tell you straight up and whatever happens, I will have to man up about it…Anthony there is not $65,000 in the bank anymore." Anthony said, "I didn't expect $65,000. Maybe about $45,000. I figured that $20,000 was spent in eight months give and take." I took a deep breath and said, "No Anthony." He looked at me and just waited. I said, "It's the opposite." Anthony was in flames! "What the hell you do?" Anthony got closer to me as tears rolled from my eyes. I looked at him and I said, "Baby, it was plenty of money about three months before you got home. I was not sure why your mother needed so much money but I could not tell your mother to stop because she just kept saying 'I'm his mother' so to me that meant for me not to ask questions." Anthony started to scream, "MOM! MOM!" and he opened the door and went to her room. It was quiet in Ms. Michelle's and waited for Anthony to return. When Anthony got back to the room he said, "My mother is coming with us." I said, "Where are we going?" Anthony said, "I'm taking you home. You don't have to. I'll take the train." I could not believe how calm he was after coming out of his mother's room. I knew that this person was not Anthony. But then again he was a momma's boy.

Anthony was a Gemini just like me and I knew his heart was

good but this was just too strange. Anthony and I were in the room and we just talked about our experience with the other people in our lives that were destroying our relationship. We agreed to always support each other's decisions. At 7:00 p.m., the sun was going down and it was time to get ready to leave. Anthony looked at me and asked if this going to be the end of our relationship. I said, "Yeah, let's depart as friends" and he agreed. Anthony said, "But I need some loving for the road." I looked at him and agreed. And we made love until dark. Anthony and I took a shower and got dressed. As I walked out the door, Anthony said "Get my mother." When I went to Ms. Michelle's room, she was going to sleep and I told Anthony but he walked in his mother's room and told her she had to ride with him. It was not over. This is when I realized that the money issue was not over. What was his plan that included his mother, I didn't know. I was now getting scared again because Anthony started to act like a nut, crazy like he had a plan that his mother and I didn't know about. Ms. Michelle had now come out the room dressed and ready to drive me home. When we got in the car, we didn't take our usual route. He went across the Crosby Bay Bridge to the Belt Parkway instead of him going through Mott Ave to the Belt towards Brooklyn and get off on Atlantic Ave. Anthony went past my stop and took the Belt to the Brooklyn Bridge. I was frantic. My heart was beating faster then I had ever felt my heart beat in my entire life. Where was he going? And what was he going to do? Anthony's mother was asleep. I was the only one that was watching what Anthony was doing, and then it came to me that he was upset that he could not accept that his money was gone. Anthony stopped the car in front of the Brooklyn Bridge. I instantly saw myself going over the bridge. When he asked me to get out of the car, I was sick to my stomach. There were so many questions that I was asking myself and I was asking God. Was he going to throw me over? Was he going to kill me first then throw me over? I just could not think straight. His mother was still asleep, like a baby, in the back seat. Anthony said, "Do you have anything to say?" I started to cry and I could not get any words to come out of my mouth. Anthony looked at me and said, "If I didn't love you, I would throw you over the bridge but you are very lucky that I really love you." I looked up at the sky and said, "THANK YOU JESUS FOR LOVING ME!" I just looked at Anthony and cried. I kept on apologizing to him about his money. I got back in the car and I was so thankful for another day.

    Anthony got in the car and took me home. He said, "If you ever need me just call." I said, "Thank you." "You have no idea how many nights I ducked and dodged the police and how much sweat and sleepless nights I had to earn my money. It's not like I go to work every week, and get a check or an annual salary. There's no pension after twenty years for me. Do you understand the tuff time, the fight and the war that comes behind this money?" I couldn't do nothing but cry and let Anthony know that I didn't know what he had been through for that kind of money. As I got out of the car, all I could do was blame myself for not being more observant about how his mother and I was spending his money. Anthony depended on me. Anthony thought more of me. He thought that I was going to be more of an investor but I failed him. Anthony dropped me off at 10:00 p.m. I went upstairs to my room and just when I thought I would have some peace in my day, my father started screaming at me about how he was tired of me in and out with Anthony and that my relationship had to end.

My father knew that Anthony could take care of me financially but my father had a problem with his daughter dealing with a man in the same life as he was. There is a saying, "What goes around, comes around." My father was a hustler. I was a little girl with everything a girl could ever want. There was nothing, I mean nothing, that I did not have. My mother came to New York City from Puerto Rico on a banana boat back in the 1950's. She was 3 years old. By the time she got to junior high school, she met my father and by the time she graduated from high school she and my father were married. They had two beautiful children, my younger brother James and I. My father gave my mother the finest things but headaches at the same time, so that's where my father saw my life heading and he didn't want me to live his life all over. He saw that in Anthony and me. Thank God for my brother being my mother's son because my brother was like my mother, worked hard and stayed out of trouble. After the screaming match and waking my mother up, I agreed to never see Anthony again. However, my dad didn't know that we ended the relationship anyway. Nonetheless, Anthony sent flowers to my job and house but I would not respond. I was daddy's little girl so I could not disappoint my father.

Two months had past since I had heard from Anthony and I was very depressed. My girlfriends were getting married and having children. I was all alone, at least that's how I felt. I was twenty-six and had no man or child. It was a bit devastating. The girls in the City were getting married and having children at my age, where did I fit in? While they were raising a family, I was a loner.

Chapter VI

New Divine Life

It was a new life for me. The next day, my depression days were over. This was easy to do when you're me; young, gifted and black with not many responsibilities. I was from Brooklyn and lived in one of the roughest neighborhoods. I was born and raised in Brownsville. Our slogan was "People from da Ville never ran and never will." For me that meant, we were strong and never ran from situations we were confronted with. My parents were from Bedford-Stuyvesant. Most people know this area of Brooklyn as "Bed-Stuy! Do or Die!" Nonetheless, how I grew up couldn't fail me. Strength was in me. I decided that it was time for me to go and get what God had in stored for me without any fear. I went to work and set a trend for myself. My goal was to work and let live. I was on a mission and it was to be a rich woman, not letting anything get in my way. If a man were to come into my life, I would deal with him differently than the way I had handled my first love.

For about two months after my breakup with Anthony, I was focused. Off I went to my job each day and back home. I had become the adult that I should have been in a long time ago. I definitely felt myself maturing. One morning, I was on my way to work and a guy sat next to me on the train and he said hello so I said hi back. He went on to say, "I have been watching you for two months and you are as serious as cancer when you get on the train." I didn't know what to make of his remark. I said, "Well, that is who I am." He then asked me for my name and I said, "Rafaela" and he replied, "I'm Divine."

"Hi Divine!"

"Would you mind if we got to know each other?"
I said, "That would be nice but I'm on my way to work."
"So I am."
"So I guess we both are not available to get to know one another."
Divine said, "Well, can I have your number?"
This time I was smarter about the situation then the time in the car when I first met Anthony and he was suppose to be taking my number and giving it to Premo. I gave Divine my beeper number and told him to page me after 6:00 p.m.
It was time for me to get off the train and I said bye to Divine and went off to work. While on my way to work, I couldn't stop thinking about this Divine guy. There was something that had me already very interested in him. He was a fine dark skinned brother, about 5'9" with pretty sparkling white teeth and he smelled good. The blacker the berry, the sweater the juice, and right about now I wanted some of that juice. He was someone I wouldn't mind getting to know.
After work, I went to see my friend Rosie. I could not wait to tell her about the fine black man I had met that morning. Rosie instantly knew something was up with me, "You have a smirk on your face." I said, "Girl...I meet this guy today on the train."
"So what happened?"
I said, "Nothing."
"You are smirking for something."
"No, he was just fine girl but I didn't go out with him or anything.
It's just strange when you are not expecting to meet anyone and you do."
Rosie asked, "So now what?"
"I told him to call me at six o'clock"
"I hope you did not give your home number out."
I said, "Are you stupid? Not so my father could be screaming."
Rosie said, "You go girl!"
After leaving Rosie's, I headed home to wait for Divine to page me. I was hopeful that my beeper would go off soon. At about 6:00 p.m., my house phone rang and it was Rosie she said, "Did he call?" "No, it's 6:00 p.m. and you're calling." Rosie said, "My bad. I will call you later."
At 6:15 p.m., my beeper vibrated and noticed that it was an unfamiliar number so I automatically knew it would be Divine. I called the number back.
"Hello! Did someone call Rafaela from this number?"

A male voice responded, "Hello!"
I said, "Hi! Who is this?"
The voice on the other end asked, "So you don't know my voice?"
"It sounds familiar but this is not a guessing game."
"It's Anthony."
My heart dropped. I could not breathe. I was speechless. He was the last person I expected to be calling me from the unfamiliar number. Anthony said, "Were you expecting my beep or someone else?" I was paralyzed on the other side of the telephone. Anthony said, "I was going through memory lane right about now." "Anthony, is this why you are calling me? I will call you back" and I hung up.

This was not happening to me. I still loved the man. I was trying to get him out of my system. My beeper vibrated again and I noticed another unfamiliar number. I said to myself this has to be Divine. I immediately called back and said, "This is Rafaela. Did anyone beep me?" "Yeah, it's Divine."

"Hi" I said with a bit of an attitude.
"What's wrong?" he asked.
"Nothing Divine."
"You are speaking like you're in distress"
I said, "It was the last call I received…It was my ex-man and I have not heard from him in three months."
"Well every man has an intuition that someone is about to take he woman of there life away."
I just laughed and said, "That was cute."
Divine said, "I'm glad that I could make you smile."

Divine and I spoke on the phone for about two hours. We chatted about a lot of different things such as life and our past relationships. I told him about what happened with Anthony. After our lovely conversation, we decided to meet in the morning before work at Broadway Junction.

The next morning, I had met with Mr. Divine at Broadway Junction and we got on the A train together. We spoke some more, this time about his goals and intentions with me. I told Divine what I expected out of a man in a relationship and he explained what he expected out of a woman. We both agreed that we would take it slow being that we both had very intense relationships in the past. When it was time for me to get off, Divine mentioned that he would beep me later and we parted.

Later that day, while on my way home from work, I saw Divine.
"What are you doing on the train," I asked. He said, "I got off

early. I wanted to see you."

I thought that it was a nice gesture on his part. Divine asked if he could take me home and I said okay. While engaged in conversation, I asked where did he live and he said, "I live on Halsey St. in Brooklyn," which was the next stop on the train we were on. I suggested that we should go chill at his house and he agreed. I made the suggestion because after receiving the random phone call from Anthony, I was afraid that he might have been waiting for me after work at the stop I get off on to go home. Anthony was so unpredictable. I don't know what he was planning for me after I didn't call him back yesterday. I had been with Anthony for four years and I knew that he would not give up on me so easily so I didn't want to take any chances. I felt confident that he would not hurt me but he would not like a man around me. He's one of those people where he felt if he couldn't have me then no one else should. I did not want to involve Divine in something he had no control over. Besides, I didn't know Divine's strengths. Anthony would throw down and take over and handle any situation in the streets. I think that's one of the reasons why I loved him so much. He was my protector. I didn't have to worry about anything with him. He was like my father. When I walked the streets with my father, I did not have to worry. I know that every woman wants a man to protect them. Regardless of the fact, Divine lived by himself so we could get a chance to know each other. There was no way he was coming up in my house so we could chill. There would have been no privacy.

Believe it or not, I was a bit frightened of the fact that he lived alone. I guess that's because I have always had my parents with me under the same roof. Regardless of the headaches, I chose to live with them (aside from the short period I stayed with Gene). It was funny that in my days, I was 26 years old and not use to a man with his on place. My parents were there and Anthony's parents were there, so to be in a house that had no rules was scary. Divine asked me if I wanted something to drink. Among the choices were champagne, wine, or soda. I did not know if this was a test or if he wanted to know if I was a drinker.

I said, "Soda please."
Divine said, "Do you drink soda all the time?"
"Yes, unless I'm out in a club. I may drink Moet."
"Wow! Big spender," he replied.
"Well, that's all I know."
"Well, I get your Anthony was a money man."
I said, "He did not drink."
Divine asked, "So how you know what's good?"

"Anthony, in the beginning of our relationship, took me out and always ordered that for me so I like it. That's the only thing I drink."

"That's the Brooklyn in you."

Divine poured my drink and also grabbed a bottle of champagne that just happened to be Moet. I said, "What you know about Moet?" He said, "I'm a man and I like to drink good too." Before sitting, he grabbed another bottle and it was Hennessey. I asked Divine, "So why are you bringing this bottle out for?" He said, "That Moet is a lady's drink. Men drink Hennessey." "Oh.....!" "Don't play yourself," I said and we both laughed.

Divine poured me a drink and he poured himself a drink and we just talked about our day and what were our future plans in life. I enjoyed getting to know each other. Time flew by and by the time I looked, it 10:00 p.m. I said, "Divine, I gotta' go home so I will call you when I get there." Divine said, "No. Let me take you home. It's late. I don't want you going by yourself." What a gentleman I thought.

I'm glad Divine decided to take me home because I was defiantly under the influence (I was very much under the influence of alcohol). I totally forgot about the possibility of Anthony roaming around looking for me. I had forgotten about the call that I had received the night before. Divine and I got on the J train to go to my house and I had not been feeling well from the liquor that I had drunk at his house. Divine took me to my door and I told him I'd see him in the morning.

Several weeks went by, and I had not heard from Anthony. I felt good as though I had started a new life with a man that understood my needs as a working woman in the world that I was living in. I was working and so was Divine. By now, it was the spring of 1989 heading into summer and Divine and I were on the J train going home from work. Since our first date, Divine had waited for me at Broadway Junction each day. This particular day, I was telling Divine what I wanted to do for the summer and asked him about his plans. Instead of answering the question Divine asked, "When was the last time you spoke to Anthony?" I said, "It's been a while." He asked me the same question again, as if he didn't believe me. I replied, "Why would you ask me that?

"I am really feeling you Fita."

"I am feeling you too."

Divine said, "It's been five month that we have been seeing each other and I would like for it to go further."

"Divine, so what is the question for?"

"I needed to know that I have you; all of you."

"You do," I said.

"I hope that you are through with him."

It was that conversation that made me realize that Divine had some insecurities about our relationship. Divine and I went to dinner that evening. We had such a great time. It was about nine o'clock when we decided to call it a night. Divine took me home and I kissed him goodnight. At about 10:30 p.m., my house phone rang and I picked it up and said, "Yes Divine." The voice on the other end said, "Oh! That's his name!? I asked, "Who is this?" The voice said, "It's Anthony!" Here we go, I thought to myself.

"Hello Anthony!"

"How are you?"

"Good, thank you."

Anthony said, "So you are seeing Divine?"

"Yes" I replied.

"Who is he?"

"You don't know him."

Anthony asked, "How did you meet him?"

"On the train about nine months ago."

I said, "No. He was just someone that I saw every morning when I got on the train at the time and he always spoke and greeted me good morning."

"So you call him your man?"

"So you were seeing him when we were together?"

"Anthony, why would you question me when every time Becky cries you run to her rescue. That's how you lost me. I guess you thought that I was going to be there for you every time the hoe stopped crying. Anthony your problem is that Becky was your little virgin girl and when she cries you think that you are her 'god.' But that chic is just tricking you. Anthony, it was different for me. When I met you, I was already a 'made woman.' She was a little girl in college with a part-time job, with dreams of becoming a lawyer. I was your woman. That's the difference. I didn't know that when you quoted these words before. I understand them now but it's too late". Anthony said, "It's not too late," and hung up.

As I hung up the phone, I was not sure what our conversation meant for Anthony so I could not go to sleep as fast as I wanted to. When I was getting ready for work the next morning, the phone rang. I picked it up before my parents would get to it. "Hello!" It was Anthony.

"What is your problem?" I said.

"YOU!"

I just laughed. Anthony went on to asks, "Is lunch good?"

I said, "No!"

"I will pick you up in front of George Westinghouse at 4:30 p.m." and he hung up.

I just ignored Anthony and went to work, meeting my man at the train station. I said, "Divine, I'm going to meet my mother today after work so I will call you when I get home." Divine said, "Okay baby. I will call you when I get in. We kissed and departed until we spoke later that day.

My day at work was the usual. I was first at my post checking ID's, then off to the cafeteria. The day moved quickly, and was already four o'clock by the time I checked my watch. After my shift, I went into the locker room to change and when I was done, I stepped out of the high school building to find Mr. Anthony already outside waiting for me in his ride. I just shook my head at him and laughed.

Anthony said, "What is so funny?"

I said, "You" and jumped in the car to head for Far Rock.

Anthony and I walked in his house and never felt so uncomfortable. I never had to change, I was always myself. Typically, very comfortable but it was different now. The way I was with Divine was different than the way I was with Anthony.

Anthony said, "I need to talk to you."

"About what?" I asked.

"What up with you and Divine?"

"That's not your question."

Anthony said, "You know my real question."

"Yes."

"Yes, as in you're sleeping with him or yes if that's my question?"

I turned towards Anthony and said, "No, I didn't sleep with him and yes that was your question."

Anthony whipped the sweat off of his forehead and I asked,

"Anthony, you are just worried about someone else sleeping with me."

For a moment, I had forgotten that Anthony's world was different than the world that Divine and I lived in. Anthony was a hustler and he couldn't fathom the thought of the woman he loves or use to love was with another man sexually. Anthony must have forgotten that I was not his woman anymore so he had no say so in what I chose to do and not to do anyway.

I said, "Anthony, what do you expected from me? I have gone on with my life. When I'm ready, I will make love to Divine; when the time is right."

Anthony said, "So the time is not yet?"

I said, "No. It's too soon. I don't want to make a mistake. I want to find true love."

"Anthony did not give you true love?" he asked.

"I don't think if you have given me true love that I would be with Divine."

Anthony looked at me and said, "Are you with Divine?"

"Yes!" I replied.

"No. I don't look like Divine."

"Anthony, because I agreed to meet with you don't mean that I'm with you."

"You know that this is what that means."

As Anthony made this statement, he began to approach me and laid some kisses on my neck that turned into sucking. HE'S PUTTING HICKIES ON MY NECK! What am I suppose to tell Divine when I see him tomorrow? I can't see him tomorrow. As I'm pondering about Divine, Anthony began to caress me. He knew how I felt about him and that I had not slept with a man since our break-up. Man, did his touch feel good. Anthony laid me down on the bed and kissed my body from top to bottom. Anthony made me so hot that I felt like I was on fire. I just needed him to take me. Away Anthony took me to another planet. He was so big and thick that it drove me crazy. As you could tell, I was his freak on the low. As he stuck his package inside of me, I just went into coma. He was always gentle, little by little, until it was fully inside of me and then I burst. It was like nothing I ever felt before. We made love like we never made love before. Anthony worked me until I was restless; like J-Holiday's song "I'ma' put you to bed."

After our episode, I woke up at midnight to call home. I told my parents that I was staying out and would go home after work. My mother asked about my whereabouts and I told her I was at Anthony's. She was pretty okay with it and didn't question me. I told her I loved her and hung up the phone. I had never told my parents that Anthony and I were not together. They never knew that we broke up, they just though that Anthony was out of town. At 3:00 a.m., my beeper began to ring consistently. It was Divine. I looked at my beeper quickly and I turned it off. Anthony said, "Is that your man? You know that it is over between you and Divine?" I said, "You have to give me time." "Okay. One month." "Okay," I said and we went back to sleep. At 6:00 a.m., I jumped out of bed and to get my clothes together. I noticed that Anthony kept my old cloths in his house. He never got rid of them.

I then got into the shower and there was a knock. "Who is that?" I asked. "Girl! It had better been you," said Ms. Michelle. "I just heard my shower and I was coming to see who it was. I had looked in Anthony's room and saw he was sleep. You coming to dinner?" she

asked. "I don't know. I have to straighten something out," I replied.
"Okay! I guess you are running late so I'll leave you to get ready." I got
out the shower and went in the room to get dressed. Next, I woke up
Anthony, "I'm going baby." Anthony said, "Call me when you get to
work." "Okay," and I left.

I hopped on the A train and noticed Divine coming from the
opposite side of the train tracks. I didn't say anything to him though. I
don't think he noticed me. When I got to work, I changed into
my uniform and headed to my daily post. I was happy that day. I was at
ease as if I had been reformed. I felt good and stress free just thinking
about my time with Anthony the night before. I couldn't face Divine yet,
so following work, I went to Rosie's house before I went home to speak
to my parents because I knew that they would not be home until 7:00
p.m. I had a bunch of hickeys on my neck. I couldn't approach Divine
that way. Besides, Divine was so insecure about our relationship and in
himself that I didn't want to prove him right. Before I could say
anything, Rosie noticed the hickeys.

"I know that you are not sleeping with Divine?" she said.

"No!" I replied.

"For a vampire to hit you like that it must have been Anthony."

"You are right!"

Rosie said, "That is some bull, so you don't go to see Divine
until those go away. Anthony thinks he's slick."

"Yeah!"

"So you two talked about the nonsense?"

I said, "Yes."

Rosie said, "So when are you going to tell Divine that it's over?"

"I have a month."

"Anthony's going to stick out that long?"

"No, you know that I will be seeing Anthony from now on. I
will just have to avoid Divine for about a week until these hickeys go
away," I said.

"Pimpin' ain't easy!!!" said Rosie.

"Look I'm going to need you to call me on the telephone at
about 9:00 p.m. tonight."

Rosie asked, "What is your plan?"

I grinned and I said, "I know that Divine will be asking me to go
to his house and I need you, Ms. Rosie, to call in and pretend like there's
an emergency with her."

My best-friend of course agreed and then I left. When I got
home, my parents were sitting in the living and my mom asked, "Oh!
Anthony's home?" I said yes and then went directly up to my room.

While I was walking into my bedroom, my mother yelled, "Your friend Divine called last night before you called to tell your father and I that you were in Anthony's house." I just yelled back and said, "Thanks mom!" At eight o'clock my house phone rang and my mother picked up and said, "Fita, it's Anthony."

"Hey poppy!" I said.

Anthony asked, "How was work?"

"Good thanks."

"What are you doing?"

I said, "Lying down on my bed. I 'm trying to regroup from my heavy ronde-vu last night."

Anthony just laughed and said, "I put your freak butt to sleep."

I said, "Yeah and you say that to say what?"

"I got to make a run. You want to come?"

"No baby. Call me when you get back."

I knew that the run meant he was going to pick up money and check his business out. I knew that it could take longer than one hour and I had to play this game right with Divine at nine. At 9:00 p.m., my telephone rang. "Hello Divine!" "Hey sexy!" he replied. I said, "Hey!"

"Are you coming over?"

"Yes. Do you need…" The telephone clicked so I said, "Hold on baby. It's someone on the other line…Hello…" It was Rosie.

"Am I on time?"

"Yeah silly! You almost blew it up."

Rosie said, "Hang up and call me back!"

When I clicked back over to the other line, I said "Divine?" and began to cry. He said, "What's wrong?" I told him that something had happened to my best friend. Divine was very sympathetic and said, "I know how you feel about Rosie so just go over there. I will see you tomorrow." "Thank you for understanding," I said and hung up. It was done for the night. I called Rosie back laughing. "You are stupid," she said. I said hysterically laughing, "Okay! I love ya!" and hung up.

The week was busy for me so I didn't get a chance to see Divine in person but we spoke on the telephone each day. By the weekend, I was exhausted but not tired enough to not hang with my best friend. On Saturday, I went over to Rosie's and picked her up so that we could go shopping for an outfit for our evening festivities at the *Paradise Garage*. It was a slammin' club on King St. down in Manhattan near the Village. We had not been their in about four months so that night we were going to our spot.

That evening, we were having a blast. The club was jumping and we were having a good ol' time when I was dancing and bumped into a guy by mistake. "FITA?" he said. When I looked, it was Divine. "Divine? What are you doing here?" I asked.

He said, "I come here every Saturday. And you?"

"I'm a member to the Garage. I have not been here since we have been together but this is my spot. Who are you here with?"

"My boy."

"I'm here with my girl Rosie."

He said, "She's feeling better I see."

I said, "Yeah. It was one of those crises."

Divine said, "So when you ready to go let me know."

I said, "Okay!" and he walked off into the crowd.

Rosie was off getting her groove on. I tapped her and said, "You will never believe who is in the club?" Rosie said, "Who?" I said, "Divine!" She looked at me with a face like "Oh boy! You're in trouble now." I just said, "It's cool" so she asked to meet him and I said okay. I went looking for him so that I could introduce them to each other.

"Rosie, this is Divine. Divine, this is Rosie."

"It's a pleasure," said Divine.

"The pleasure is mine," Rosie replied.

After the introduction, Rosie and I headed back to the dance floor to have a good time. The night was great. I was out with my people that I haven't been with in a while, just having fun. We left the club at 7:00 a.m. and went straight to a breakfast joint. Our spot was at *Galaxy* in Brooklyn on Pennsylvania Ave and Linden Blvd. We hopped in my car and went to eat. I never did go and find Divine before I left. I just wanted to leave the club and spend some more time with my best friend. After eating my breakfast, scrabbled eggs cooked hard (I can't see the white) with bacon, toast, and homefries, we headed home. I first dropped off Rosie at her house and then went to mine.

Later that Sunday afternoon, I woke up and just relaxed at my house. At nine o'clock, Divine called. "Hello Divine!" "What up?" he asked. I said, "I'm staying in the house. I will see you in the morning on the train." Divine said okay and hung up. At 10:30 p.m. the phone rang and this time it was Anthony, "Hello Anthony!" "Did you enjoy yourself at the *Garage*?" he asked. In a sexy voice I replied, "Yes baby, I will talk to you tomorrow. Okay?" Anthony said, "No, come downstairs. I'm in front of the door." So I hung up the phone and rushed to the bathroom to brush my teeth and wash my face, and then went downstairs. I opened the door and Anthony said, "You know I have not seen you in a few days so write a note to mommy and daddy letting them know that you are at my house." I grinned and headed back inside my house to write the note, which I left on the dining room table.

After gathering some of my belongings, Anthony and I headed to the Rockaways. Of course the night was good, my man made love to me. Every time I'm with Anthony, it's different. This time it was like I was hungry and he was the only man that had the necessary food to feed me. I yearned for his comfort. The next morning I went to work hoping that the day would end sooner than it did. After a long night at the club and the time I spent with Anthony, I was exhausted. I just wanted to go home and sleep. When work was finally over, I did just that and also made sure that I didn't answer the phone. When my mom got home from work, she asked if I was okay and I assured her that things were fine with me and that I was just tired.

The phone rang and it was Divine. My mom told him that I would call him back. At 10:30 p.m. the phone rang, "I got it!" I yelled. "Anthony, I will be ready in a minute." Anthony said, "If you are tired, I will let you sleep." "Thanks baby, I want to stay home. But call me when you get home," I replied. And he did. Anthony called at about eleven o'clock to confirm his arrival to his home. "Okay, see you tomorrow," I said.

The next morning, while I was getting ready for work, the phone rang. It was Divine. I said, "I will see you in a minute" and I hung up. I got on the J train at Crescent and approached Halsey when Divine walked in and said, "Hi baby!"

I said, "What up? Why did you call the house if you knew that you would see me?"

Divine said, "It's not like I always see you on the train anymore and you don't come over my house too much anymore either."

"I have just been busy."

"Saturday you were in the club."

I said, "But you were too."

He said, "I only went cause' you didn't call me after Friday. That's the last day I spoke to you. We changed our plans because Rosie had a crisis and you didn't call anymore after that until I saw you on Saturday at the Garage."

"Divine, I didn't call you because it's been a long time since I've gone out with my best friend being that she now has two children. She does not get out much."

Divine said, "I understand."

The end of that conversation; we went on talking about Saturday evening. Divine looked at me and asked, "What up with Anthony?" I said, "He's okay. I spoke to him." "When was I going to know? I said, "Baby, you are so wrapped up with knowing so much about Anthony, I'm worried."

Divine said, "That nigga' know you are a good woman and he messed up."

"If you feel threatened, then why would you want to be with me?"

"I'm going out of town and I want to know that I have a women that I could come back home to."

I was stunned. I said, "Why are you going out of town?"

Divine said, "I have some business to take care of."

"Is it for your job?'

"Yes," he replied.

I asked, "When are you leaving?"

"Tomorrow."

I looked at him and asked, "Why so sudden?"

He said, "I have been trying to tell you for about two weeks but you have been very busy."

I asked, "For how long?"

"Two weeks so come over to my house tonight." I agreed.

It was so easy now. Before, I thought that it would be so hard in another week to break it off with Divine because my one month was running out but it didn't seem that way at that moment. I wanted to be with my man Anthony. I was always comfortable with Anthony; being with him seemed so different this time around. I could not figure it out why it seemed so different but I just wanted more and more of Anthony. I went to Divine's house and we drank and got very comfortable with each other. Next thing I knew, I was in Divine's bed. We stared to kiss and I could feel Divine's penis getting hard. It was getting bigger and bigger and I started to get horney. As Divine started to undress me, his beeper went off. I was a bit confused because I didn't know he had a beeper because I never heard it go off while we were together for all of these months. He stopped what he was doing to go answer his page. I overheard him saying that he was leaving in the morning so I thought it was someone from his job he was talking to.

When Divine walked back into the room, he asked, "May we finish what we started?" and I replied, "I don't think that is a good idea. I think if we are going to get involved like that I would like for us to wait until you get back." I know that was a low blow. Divine's face was confused. I could tell he was upset but he accepted my explanation. I said, "Baby, I'm going to leave before something happens that we both are not sure of." It was about 11:00 p.m., and I informed Divine that I would be alright going home by myself. When I got home, it was midnight and my phone rang. I quickly picked it up so that the annoying rings would not wake my parents. It was Anthony. He asked, "Where were you?"

"I was out at..."

Before I could finish my sentences, Anthony said, "With Divine."

"Yes."

"I guess you called it off."

"Yes," I replied.

"Baby, can I come and get my woman?"

I said, "Now?"

He said, "Is there a problem?" "No" I replied.

Anthony seemed like he was waiting for me to say no. He just wanted to know if I had slept with Divine. All he really wanted to do was test his pie (vagina) firsthand. If it wasn't tight, he would have known that I was having sex with Divine. Nonetheless, I waited for him to come and pick me up. I felt like the night was going to be too much for me so I decided I would call into work and take a personal day. The thought of Anthony and his love making, and the possibility of Divine asking me hundreds of questions in the morning, it was killing me. I needed some time off.

Anthony drove to my house to pick me up. Before I left, I wrote a note for my parents. The minute we got to Anthony's room, he was already hard and ready to get at it. Anthony had so much energy and I loved it. I had a lot of energy too so we always had blast with each other. Anthony undressed me and started to kiss me all over. I just wanted him hurry up and feed me and forget the foreplay. Every time he touched me, I shivered. I wanted him now, not now, but right now.

Sex was funny though. I must admit, we did compete against each other. It was always a lovemaking contest between the two of us. I would get on top and ride him until he could not think anymore. I came that night so much that my juices were pouring out onto the bedspread. Later, Anthony turned me over and rocked my world until he put me to bed. We always wanted to make sure that each of us was satisfied before we each got off for the night.

The next day was the beginning of a three day weekend for me. I hadn't called out of work in a long time. My day was spent in the Rockaways with Anthony, and on Saturday we finally decided to get out of bed. I wasn't feeling well though. I went to Ms. Michelle, "Are you alright," she asked. "I've just been feeling tried lately." Ms. Michelle thought I should go to the doctor. I replied, "I'm fine. It's just that I have been running around so much lately. My body is just tried." In the meantime, Anthony went to take care of business and returned home to get right in the bed. I told him that he needed to get up because I wanted some fish so we went out to eat.

The following weekend made five weeks since Anthony and I had been together, and it was a week before Divine would return from his two week trip. I was feeling unbalanced so I went to the doctor because my family has a history of health problems such as high blood pressure so I went to the doctor for the sole purpose of checking my pressure. Instead, the doctor came back and said that there's nothing wrong with my pressure but instead told me I was pregnant. I screamed, "THIS CAN'T HAPPEN TO ME!" The doctor said, "Yeah, you are five weeks." I took my results and ran out of the office.

This could not be happening to me. I had goals to accomplish. I remembered a discussion I had with God. I told God that he would be proud of me. I wanted to be success. I wanted to be famous. I wanted to own my own production company. I wanted to have a recording company. I wanted to become Diana Ross. I wanted to be the black Barbara Streisand. These were the things that I went to school for and I was good at it. I was a singer, dancer, and actress. Years of practice and performances in off-Broadway productions, student at Alvin Alley Dance School for ten years, and where would that all go now with a baby? I needed to speak to someone, quick–fast but not my parents; they would be devastated. All the performances they attended, all the awards and scholarships that I received, all the years' I spent in theater and music was going to go down the drain. I was confused. Why? Why God? But never once did I stop to think that if I was out there having sex with Anthony and not covering up something like this was bound to happen. I was young, stupid and extremely naive.

Today is the day; Divine is coming home and I was not the same. I had a baby growing inside of me and no one knew but me. I did not want to see Divine so I went to work and spent time with Rosie afterward. "Why do you look so bright in the face?" she asked.

"I don't know," I replied.

"Why are you sad?"

"I'm pregnant," I replied with a sad look on my face.

Rosie was surprised. She looked like she saw a ghost. I looked at Rosie and said, "I don't know what I'm going to do so don't ask." Rosie said, "Look on the brightside, you are 27 years old. Fita you are not a child. You have a good job and Anthony is a good man. He takes you every where, gives you anything you want, and the most important part is that he loves you. He has a strange way of showing it but he does. It's not like you just met him. You have been with him for years, so what's the problem?" I looked at Rosie in her big brown eyes and said, "How about me? How about my goals?" Rosie replied, "You'll have to work that out on your own."

After talking to my girl, I felt a little better. I went home and waited for Divine to call. I wanted to just get it over with and end the relationship we had. I was ready to be friends but I had to find a nice way to put it. Divine had mentioned that he was really feeling me before he left so I wanted to be gentle. The telephone rang and I answered it and it was Anthony.

"Hey mami!"

"Hey papi!"

"What are you doing?" he asked.

I said, "I'm waiting for my parents to get home. I have not spoken to them or had dinner with them all weekend."

"True dat'. True dat'."

"Papi, I will call you later."

He said, "Okay!" and hung up.

In the meantime, I decided to take a shower to kill some time before Divine called me. After lotioning-up and putting on my pajamas, I was going to lie down on my bed but the phone rang; this time it was Divine. "Hey baby!"

I said, "Hey Divine," in a very monotone voice.

"You don't sound good."

I said, "I don't feel good…How was your trip?"

"It was good but I could not wait to come back and see you."

I said, "Divine, I have to talk to you."

"Okay, can we meet?"

"No! I would like to just talk to you over the phone." He then got very quiet.

I said, "Divine, I have been seeing Anthony for about two weeks and you know that my heart's been there for a long time."

Divine said, "I'm not giving you up so we will play it by ear."

"Divine, you don't know Anthony."

"I don't care."

I said, "Divine, it is out in the open so that's on you if you not trying to give me up." Divine said, "You know that Anthony's going in and out of town at least you will have a friend you can hangout with at a movie or something."

After Divine made the friendship statement, things were cool. We stayed talking on the phone about my situation with Anthony so he could really understand how I felt about him. Following our conversation, I felt relieved. I was trying to clean up my pimp game so I felt more at ease with myself. Knowing that at any point in time I could have bumped into Divine on the street with Anthony, I would not have felt good about the situation if I didn't break it off in time. I was feeling much better. I would have hated to feel like I got caught in my game. Anthony would probably have killed me anyway, so to avoid all that I had to come clean with Divine.

By that time, the holidays were rolling around and the weather was getting colder. My thanksgiving was spent with mine and Anthony's family. Anthony didn't really go over my families place. I spent more time with his family instead. Of course me and Divine stayed friends, and it was nice having a man to speak to besides Anthony. A week before Christmas, Anthony had to go out of town. I found myself hanging out more with Diane because she was much more available than Rosie back at that time. Rosie had another child, Jhameek, back in July so she didn't go out as much. The last time we had gone out was when we went to the *Garage* and her mom babysat for her. Diane's mother, Mrs. Mott, would babysit Diane's son who was 10 years old.

The Saturday before Christmas, my telephone rang. I was half sleep after recovering from drinking and going out with Diane the night before. When I answered, I wasn't fully aware that it was Divine I was talking to in my sleep. Divine asked me if he could come to my house to bring me a Christmas gift so I agreed and told him to stop by at seven o'clock. He agreed to the time, and I hung up and went back to sleep. At about 3:00 p.m., I got up and saw a note from my parents saying they went to Junior's house to see my nieces and nephew. The telephone rang and it was Anthony.

"Hey mami!"

"Hey papi!

Anthony said, "I will be there at seven o'clock to see you and I'm bringing you your Christmas gift before I leave."

I said, "Okay papi! But we need to talk when you get here."

Anthony asked, "Mami why don't you talk to me now."

"I was going to wait until Christmas but I guess I'll let you know now."

"Okay shout (meaning tell me)," he said.

"I'M PREGNANT!" I shouted with a sudden burst of joy.

"How many months?" he asked.

"Well, I suppose that I'm two months now. I went about three weeks ago, the weekend that I was feeling sick and your mother told me to go to the doctor and that was the result."

"Okay! I'll see you at seven o'clock."

Anthony was so laid back with life and I was so in love with the way he handled life. It was not my secret anymore and I was very happy with Anthony's response. I didn't feel like I still had a knot in my stomach as I did before. I finally got it off my chest and told my baby daddy. I remembered when we got together, it was just to have fun; no marriage, and no baby was our agreement (I guess that agreement went down the drain).

I went back to sleep after speaking with Anthony and woke up at six o'clock. I was very hungry so I got up, showered, got dressed and went to Wendy's. I ate my food at the Wendy's and walked back home. By now, a half-hour had passed. It was almost time to see Anthony. When I got home, Divine called. "Hi Divine!" "Hey! I'm waiting on my man to drive me to your house," he said.

I said, "What are you talking about?"

He replied, "I called you this morning and I told you I was coming to see you to give you a gift."

"I don't remember."

"It's okay."

"Well, you could come about 8:30 p.m.," I said.

"Cool."

I was cool with him coming at that time. I knew that Anthony was going out of town so he would only be at my house for a few minutes and then get ready to leave for his trip. At seven o'clock, there was no Anthony. He didn't call so I beeped him. When he called back, he said he was on his way, he just had to make sure everyone working for him was on point. By eight o'clock, I began to get worried so I beeped him again. By then, there was a knock at the door and it was him. Anthony had finally arrived. "So you are pregnant?" he asked.

"Yes," I replied.

"Is that what you want?"

I looked at him and said, "I don't know."

Anthony said, "Is it that you don't want my baby?"

"It's not that. It's my future I'm looking at."

Anthony said, "Mami, you are my woman and that's my seed and we planted it there so while I'm on business you decide what you want. The decision is yours."

Anthony then opened up his wallet and handed me $500.00 and said, "I didn't have time to put something up so take this and Merry Christmas." Not once could he say I love you. I kissed him and he said, "Mami, I will be back next weekend on Saturday." "Okay. Be safe and don't forget to call me."

It was 9:00 p.m. and Divine had not arrived or called back so I went on to sleep. At 2:00 a.m. my phone rang; it was my man.

"Hey Anthony! What up?"

"Just thinking of you and my child."

"Mr. I have not told my parents."

Anthony said, "What are you waiting for?"

I replied, "New Years."

"Are you ashamed of having my baby?"

"No! But my parents expect so much from me. I never discussed children. Having kids was never my passion."

Anthony said in a low voice, "Okay mami, I will call you later" and he hung up.

I think Anthony was bothered by my lack of excitement. I wasn't like his little chicken-head girlfriends that he was use to, like Becky. She would have probably been all excited to be having his child. I'm scared. Kids are no joke.

The entire week, I went to work with a big grin on my face but I was not totally myself because I still had this secret awaiting announcement to my parents. My mother said on Friday night, "What's up? Is something wrong?" I said no of course. "I know that you and Anthony have been very close these few weeks. Where is he?" I said he went out of town. At that moment, something inside of me just said tell her so I said, "Mommy..." "I don't want you to make a bad decision because of your father," she replied. I looked at her and said, "What are you talking about?" I looked at my mother and I just smiled and tear rolled down my face. The secret was now out of the bag! (she had a good mother's intuition).

The next day, Anthony called and I said, "Hey Baby!" "Baby, what's wrong? Something happened to the baby?" he asked. I said, "No papi!" "Then what is so different about your voice?" "Well, I had a talk with my mother..." Anthony said, "AND?" "And she knew all along that I was pregnant and she said that I shouldn't feel like I let anyone down. The decision is yours and mine." Anthony said, "Well, I will be home in two days." I said, "Okay baby, be careful."

Chapter VII

Reunited

It was like a reunion for me. Life was treating me well. It was God that was working in my favor. It was the Saturday of Anthony's return home, and we were going to be reunited. The secret that we had was now out in the open. There were no more depressing days for us in our future. We were going to finally become a family. I knew that Anthony would be home from Pennsylvania around three o'clock so I started to get myself together. I wanted to look good for my man, especially since I was going to be a new mother. I needed to look as good as I possible; I could not slip. You know some women tend to feel fat and ugly when they get pregnant, but I refused to feel that way. At two o'clock, the phone rang.

"Hi Anthony!" I assumed.

"Hello!" the voice replied but it wasn't Anthony. It was Divine.

"Hey! How are you? I have not heard from you since last week."

Divine said, "Yeah, I know. I could not get a ride so can I come today?"

"Yeah, if you come before 3 p.m."

"I will be there about 2:30 p.m."

"Cool!" I replied.

After hanging up the phone, I rushed to finish getting dressed. I still had to do my hair. I wanted to make sure I was ready so that I didn't have to worry about doing my hair or anything else once Divine left. I already knew what Divine got me, it was a bottle of Hennessey. I don't know why he bought me liquor, like I drank like that. The gift was not that important to me but I did have a bar in my house that was always full just in case guests came over. My parents and I always made sure we could entertain our company with a variety of drinks. Nevertheless, I was raised to not turn down a gift. The fact that someone is offering it to me, it was a nice gesture so to be nice, I would accept it.

The telephone rang again, "Mami, I'm in the city. I will be there soon," said Anthony. I said okay and hung up. The phone rang again and this time it was Divine calling me back to tell me he was on his way. It was now 2:40 p.m., and I was still waiting on Divine. My plan was that he would get to my house by 2:30 p.m., and drop off the bottle and leave before Anthony got to my house. At 3:00 p.m., Divine finally called me to say he was downstairs and asked that I go downstairs and open the door. When I opened the door, Divine handed me the gift all nicely wrapped. He did such a good job, I just had to smile. Divine smiled back and I invited him up to my apartment. I placed the bottle on the living room table and we sat on the couch.

Divine asked, "So how are things going with Anthony?"

"Good thanks!"

"Are you and Anthony planning on moving in together?"

"What are you talking about?" I replied. Before I could say anything else, the phone rang and it was Anthony.

"Hey mami! Open the door."

I instantly got nervous and began to stutter, "Are...are... you...uhm...downstairs?"

Anthony said, "Yeah, is something wrong?"

I didn't know what exactly to say, "Uhh..."

Anthony asked, "What? You have company?"

I was honest and said, "Yes."

"Who? Divine upstairs?"

"Yes."

"Okay, open the door. I'd be pleased to meet Divine."

I hung up the phone and looked at Divine. He already knew what the deal was. I said nothing and hurried downstairs to open the door. I didn't want to keep Anthony waiting and have him think more was going on upstairs than what was really happening, which was nothing. Divine and I were just talking. When I opened the door, Anthony barged in and ran directly upstairs to see who Divine was. I slammed the door and ran up behind him. When Anthony walked into the house, he said with a cool voice, "What is up Divine?" and walked over to slap him five. Anthony went on to say, "I have not seen you since the stick up. It was about two years ago." What the hell? What is going on here? I was stunned. Here I am running up behind Anthony because I thought he was going to hurt Divine but they actually knew each other. Divine and Anthony were stickup buddies a while back. I looked at Anthony and he looked at me and said, "Fita, you keep forgetting that I have family in Brooklyn. Because I live in Queens does not mean that I don't know people in Brooklyn." I just stared at the both of them in awe.

"Divine, go to my car with my cousin Dinkie and I will take you home," Anthony insisted. "Let me speak to my girl." I could not believe that Divine left me there. I thought to myself, "Well, bye to you too, stupid." I felt Divine had no balls for a man. I was pissed off and speechless.

Anthony asked, "So what were you and Divine going to get into?"

"Nothing, he was just bringing me a bottle."

"What for?" Anthony said angrily.

I said, "It was a gift."

"A gift for what?"

I explained, "Divine is still my friend…"

"So why would a friend bring a woman that has a man some liquor for? To get you drunk and to have sex with you."

I rolled my eyes and said, "Who do you think I am? First of all…"

Anthony chimed in, "Right! First of all, he should not be bringing a woman that is carrying a baby no kind of alcohol. Why didn't he just bring orange juice or something? Is this what you want?"

As he said this, he reached out and ripped my shirt open. I stood in front of him shocked. I didn't know what to do. We were in the living room when he grabbed me and ripped the rest of my clothes off and began humping me. He was doing it so hard it began to hurt me. I was scared. As he continued to hump me viciously, he kept on saying over and over, "Is this what you want? Is this what you want?" For a moment, I felt like his whore, not his woman or the woman that was going to have his baby. I froze like a rape victim, refusing to participate in the sexual act. When Anthony got up after he ejaculated in me, he said "I will be back. I'm going to take care of some business." I couldn't move. I was in complete shock.

He left and I felt awful. I was home alone. My parents were at my brother's for the weekend so I decided I needed to leave. I was not going to take any chances and stay home in case Anthony decided to return. At that point, I didn't know if he was angry enough to hurt me. I put on some clothes, called a cab, and fleeted to my girlfriend Diane's house. She lived in Prospect Plaza in Brownsville. I refused to be on the front page of the Daily News or the New York Post the next morning. The situation was crazy. One minute my man was excited to be returning home to see me, and the next minute I was his enemy. I didn't know what was happening to us. I didn't know what Anthony was going to do to me or to Divine but I was not going to stick around to find out. I jetted out of my house and hopped inside of the taxi-cab. I was nervous. I couldn't help not to think that Anthony was somewhere hiding and would follow the cab to my destination. I began rambling to the cab driver about what happed. I'm sure he thought I was crazy but I needed to vent to someone and he was my only outlet at that time. I got up the hill, known a Prospect Plaza; I threw my money at the cab driver and dashed into the building. I slid my way into the closing elevator door and headed to the 10th floor. When I got there, I hurried to Diane's apartment and rang the doorbell saying, "Mrs. Mott open the door!" Mrs. Mott opened the door with a slight attitude, "Girl, what's wrong with you?" I would have rolled my eyes and sucked my teeth too if someone came to my door ringing the doorbell like a maniac, and demanded me to open the door like they pay rent at my place. Ignoring her attitude, I replied with hesitance, "Mrs. Mott, I think Anthony is going to hurt my friend Divine. Mrs. Mott I was in the house and I was waiting on Anthony but my friend called to give me a late Christmas gift and Anthony came in and you know how he is..." Mrs. Mott said, "I think you need a drink. Go in the room. There is some Bacardi." I wasn't thinking. I totally forgot about the baby. I was just scared. My nerves were "shot." I didn't realize what I was doing. I grabbed the bottle and took a sip, and then another. Soon after, I got sick and threw up. Mrs. Mott said, "You sick like that off of Bacardi." She looked at her bottle and said, "Fita, you drunk up the Johnny Walker Black." I drank the wrong drink and didn't even realize it until Mrs. Mott pointed it out to me. I was in a "zone."

After I threw up, I got myself together and took a cab to the club that Ms. Mott said Diana was bartending at that night. The place was on Herzl and Strauss in Brooklyn. We called it the 308 Club. It was an after hour spot and people had to be over 25 years old to get in. When I got there, I was already drunk. I couldn't face what had happened with me and my man; the love of my life. I found Diane and chilled with her at the bar until 3:00 a.m., and then I decided to go home. Thank God my parents were home. I had no fear when my parents were around because Anthony would never disrespect my parents so I knew I was going to be okay. When I entered the house, I didn't realize that I made so much noise that it caused my father to wake up.

"Sorry, daddy. Uhm! If any body calls, I'm sleep."
"What?"
"I said of anyone calls, tell them I'm sleep."

"Okay but if you are up to some games with your little boyfriend, I'm not getting involved 'Ms. Pimpette,'" he laughed.

"No daddy, I'm tired. I was hanging out with Diane and I just need so sleep."

My father said, "Okay!"

"But please tell mommy the same. Thanks daddy."

My mother was my girl. She would go along with my games. At 11:00 a.m., Divine called. "What the hell do you want? You left me for dead with Anthony."

Divine said, "I can't believe that you two were really together."

"What did you think that I was lying?"

"I need to talk to you," said Divine.

I didn't want to be bothered so I just hung up.

Divine called back. "Just leave me alone," I said.

"I really need to talk to you. It's something that you need to know."

I said, "What Divine?"

"I need to see you face to face."

"Okay, fine. I will meet you at Wendy's on Atlantic Ave and Logan St."

"What time?" Divine asked.

I said, "About five o'clock."

"Okay, thanks," he said and hung up. This would give me plenty of time to get myself together.

When I got up from my bed and walked out of my bedroom, my father asked who I was speaking with. I said Divine. My father seemed concerned and asked me what happened. Because me and my dad had a pretty open relationship, I decided to tell him what had happened the day him and my mom was not home, minus the disturbing sexual encounter with Anthony.

My father said, "What is wrong with you? Why did you have Divine up here knowing that Anthony was coming?" "Daddy, I did not think that it was going to trn out the way it did. Divine was just suppose to bring me the gift and go. Plus, it was at 2:30 p.m. and Anthony was coming home at 3:00 p.m…" My dad interrupted, "You are no little girl. You know what you are doing but you need to make a decision, and stop dragging them along and let one go." My father knew that the life I was living was dangerous but I took after him. A hustler's daughter stays in deep stuff. "Daddy, I'm with Anthony. Divine is just a friend." My Father said, "But Divine seems to want more and he is getting in your way so you need to shut him down. You are having a baby. Did you forget? And Anthony is not going to let no other man around you so you need to get your act together." He continued, "Well, as long as my baby girl doesn't get hurt, I'm fine. But if she does get hurt, one of those sorry ass young men will have to see me." Following the conversation with my dad, I began to dress for my meet with Divine.

Today was New Year Eve's of 1988, and I was at Wendy's restaurant on Atlantic Ave and Howard Ave, while everyone in the world was getting ready to go out for the holiday. Divine arrived right five o'clock like we agreed. I got right to the point, "So what's so important that you needed to see me today?"

Divine said, "I don't want you to be mad and I don't need you to repeat this to Dee."

I agreed and I said, "So what up?"

"Well I am sorry for what happened the other night..."I just listened. "Well the other day when I was suppose to come to your house I did not have a ride so I asked my man to drive me to your house but I was in the pink houses (project apartment) in Brooklyn on Linden Blvd. My man's name is Dinkie. Dinkie did not know where he was going to drop me off at but he said he would drop me off as soon as his cousin Dee got to the building. Since I had not seen Dee in about two years, I said ok. I began asking about Dee and Dinkie said he was cool and that on his way dropping me off, he planned on dropping his cousin Dee off to his girl's house on Crescent St. So that's when I asked Dinkie on Crescent and what. Dinkie responded Crescent and Fulton. Then I asked what Dee's girl's name was. Dinkie said her name is Fita. Then that's when my eyes got wide and Dinkie said do you know her and I responded yeah, I think I do. Dinkie said well where you are going on Crescent and that's when I said well I'm going to Crescent and before I could say anything else Dee was on the scene. I slapped him five and gave him a brotherly hug. Dee hugged his cousin and Dee said, 'Come on Dinkie, I have to go see my girl.' Dinkie said, 'I want to drop Divine off because he has been waiting for me to drop him off to some girl's house.' Then Dee said well where are you going Divine and I said I'm going on Crescent and Fulton. Dee looked at me and said where and before I could say anything Dee asked me if I'm the Divine that was seeing his girl Fita. I said yeah but I told him that I did not know that he was Anthony because I didn't know his birth name until that day. Dee then went on to say, 'You know that she's having my baby.' I said no I did not know that you were pregnant. When we arrived, Dee told me to go upstairs first. Just so you know Fita, we came together in Dinkie's car. After the situation had happened and he said for me to go to his car, it was Dinkie's car and Dee did not want to throw you off and did not want you to know Dinkie was downstairs. Dee wanted to see how you would react, so Dee called all the shots. Not for one moment would I have matched that your Anthony was Dee Nice, Master Dee. I guess I asked for that. I wanted to know so badly who Anthony was. "

I asked, "Divine but why did you play the game?"

Divine said, "I'm sorry! I will not bother you anymore. What are you going to do for the New Year?"

I said, "I will be spending the New Year with my family and then I will be with Dee's family tomorrow."

"You are going over there!"

"Yeah. And?" I said with an attitude.

Divine said, "It's like that?"

"It is," I replied.

"You go over there without Dee?"

"Yes. I stay with his mother."

Divine said, "Isn't Dee going back out of town?"

"Yes."

"So you will stay there?"

"Yeah."

Divine continued with his questions, "You could go there without Dee?"

I said, "Divine, I use to live there."

Divine said, "No... It's not like that."

This boy obviously was not listening to me, "WHATEVER!" I said and I left.

That evening I went home very upset. I couldn't believe that Anthony set me up. No doubt Dee gets respect by his people and the little chicks out in the street that got his head gassed. He swears he's the man. I didn't give a heck about how other people viewed and respected him. He obviously thought he could do whatever he wanted and would get away with it but that was not the case. I was going to get his butt back.

The New Year's ball had dropped and it was the beginning of a new time in my life. I was supposed to be on my way to Anthony's house on January 1, 1989 but I was still home. I had received my first call and it was Anthony. He was on the telephone speaking to my father wishing him a happy New Year, and then he asked to speak to my mother. After wishing her a happy New Year as well, I got on the phone.

"Happy New Year Baby!" Anthony said excitingly.

I said, "Thank you but I need to have a word with you before you go out of town."

"Anything mami."

"Why would you have to set me up like that?"

Anthony said, "First of all, you are having a baby and you need to get yourself together."

"Wait minute; YOU need to get yourself together. I have my stuff done."

Anthony said, "Look, just get your butt over here before I go out of town."

"When are you going?"

"I leave tomorrow."

I said, "Well how long are you staying?" Anthony said for two days and that would be the last time he would be traveling out of town for work ever again. I said "Well, we will talk about this stuff when you come back." Anthony said, "When I come back, your butt better be at my house."

I said, "Okay." and I hung up.

Well, I didn't go. Two days had gone by and the telephone rang, it was Anthony.

He asked, "Why are you still there?"

I said, "I was getting myself together."

"Oh well! If you are not at my house by the time I get in the city, I'm coming to get you." The nerve of Anthony; he said he was coming to get me because my parents did not know how to watch me, as though I was a child. "Anthony I am grown."

"If they knew how to watch you this stuff wouldn't have happened," said Anthony.

At five o'clock, Anthony called back. "What up? Why are you not here?" I was a bit scared of his tone and just about the entire situation that happened before he had left so I was kind of nervous to go over, aside from trying to teach him a lesson about how he ain't all that.

Anthony said, "Just be downstairs in about 20 minutes. Fita let me talk to daddy."

I said, "He's not home."

"Then let me speak to mommy."

"Hold on." I yelled for my mom to pick up the phone.

"Happy New Year mommy," Anthony said again.

"The same to you, Anthony."

"Mommy you know I'm coming to get Fita."

Mommy said, "Yeah. What's the problem?"

Anthony said, "Well before I left mommy, Fita had a man up in your house drinking liquor."

"What?"

"Yes! So we have to talk mommy, because that is not what she should be doing."

Mommy said, "I know she was not drinking Anthony."

"No but she had a man in your house and she is suppose to be with me."

"That's something that you two need to talk about." As soon as my mother hung up, the doorbell rang and it was Anthony. My mom let him in, while in the meantime I called Ms. Michelle to let her know that I was on my way to her house, in case I didn't make it then she would call my mother.

Ms. Michelle said, "What is going on? Anthony left here so angry?"

"Ms. Michelle, I will tell you when I get there. I should be there in about 20 minutes."

I went downstairs and we both said, "Happy New Year" to each other; then Anthony and I got in his car and headed for Far Rock. As we approached Bay Towers, my stomach started feeling funny. When we pulled up to the garage, it seemed extra spooky. While walking to the building, Anthony's beeper went off. He looked at the number and when we got upstairs, he went directly to his room and got something and said to his mother and myself, "I will be back," and he just left.

About five minutes after Anthony had left, his house phone rang and I picked up and said hello but the person on the other end hung up.

Ms. Michelle asked, "Who was that?"

I shrugged my shoulders and said, "They just hung up." The phone rang again.

I said, "Hello!" The person on the other end was just breathing heavily on the phone but did not respond. "Hello! Hello!"

Ms. Michelle said, "Who's that?"

"I don't know."

"What do they think, this is a spot?" (meaning the caller was looking for some product from Anthony). The caller hung up again.

"HELLO!" I said for the third time picking up the phone. There was silence on the other end. "Hello Fita!" the voice finally replied.

"Yes?" The voice was familiar to me.

"I can't believe that you answer the phone as though you live there," now I recognized the voice.

I said, "Divine? What are you doing calling here?"

Divine said, "The night that Dee brought me home, we exchanged numbers and I was suppose to meet him today."

"Well, he not here."

"I would have never believed that the relationship was that

deep."

I said, "Well Divine, what did you expect?"

He said, "The way Dee was talking about you, I did not think it would that deep."

"Well maybe he wants to save face being that you were actually going to see his baby's mother and he didn't want to make it seem like he was sprung!"

Divine said, "I will never bother you again."

I said, "Thank you!" and hung up the telephone.

Ms. Michelle asked, "Who was that?"

It as time for me to tell Ms. Michelle what had happen before Anthony went out of town. After that phone conversation, I never did speak to or saw Divine.

At approximately 4:00 a.m., Anthony crawled in bed, "Where were you?" I asked. "I had to take care of something," he replied. "Well, we need to talk." "Can't we talk in the morning?" "Okay, but in the morning," I replied and turned over and went back to sleep.

A few hours later, I woke Anthony up I said, "Anthony we have to talk because Divine called here." Anthony opened his eyes and said nonchalantly, "He won't ever bother us again." Anthony's facial expression and tone of voice sounded as if Divine was nonexistent. It was bothersome to me, "What did you do?" "Nothing," he replied.

One week later, Anthony asked me to attend a funeral with him for one of his people's that had recently passed. When we arrived in front of the funeral parlor, Anthony told me to stay in the car. I did not understand why Anthony invited me and didn't want me to see the body. As people exited the funeral parlor, I noticed a few women that I knew, so I asked the group of women who were they there to see and they responded Divine. I then asked if they had seen Anthony and one of the girls directed me to the front of the funeral parlor. One of the girls Angel asked, "Why are you in the car? I responded, "I can't take funerals…Hey! Do you have an obituary?" Angel stretched out her arm to pass me the document, "Here, I don't know if you knew him." I looked at the picture on the front cover and my heart stopped. It was really Divine; my Divine. The women were starring at me and I said, "No. I did not know him." I thanked Angel and I got out of the car to enter the funeral.

I stormed directly to the front of the funeral parlor where Anthony was with his people and I said, "Can I have a word with you?" "Okay baby, one minute," he said as he shook his peoples hand and proceeded to the car. When we entered the vehicle, I said, "WHY?!" with a confused face. Anthony said, "Why what?" "Anthony, how did

Divine die?" Sarcastically Anthony replied, "Divine broke some rule to the game." "What game?" I asked. Anthony said, "It's nothing you should be concerned with," and the conversation was left at that.

Chapter VIII

Missing Divine

As time passed and we tried putting Divine behind us, our relationship turned sour. Our relationship started going downhill again when Anthony started going out of town with his "business" a lot more, while I stayed home. Anthony was hustling hard and I kept busy at work. When he was home, Anthony and I would go out to eat and see a movie from time to time but we didn't seem to enjoy our relationship like we had in the past. I guess things also changed after I decided to have an abortion. With all the drama that occurred during my pregnancy, I didn't think that the baby would be okay when born. I was depressed for a very long time as a result of my decision.

The year went by, and Anthony and I didn't see each other much. It was like this frequently, there were months we were very close and others when we were distant; that is how the business affected us. Once, Anthony was gone for about three weeks before he had called to tell me he was finally returning home. I wasn't sure why his business trips needed to take so long, and what were some things he may have been getting into but I didn't ask and Anthony definitely didn't tell. He kept most things to himself. Nonetheless, initially I was blind to a lot of what was going on and at other times I just chose to ignore them.

The day that Anthony called, I patiently waited for him to arrive. Hours past, and no response from Anthony as to whether or not he got home safely so I called his house and Ms. Michelle said that Anthony had been home about two days. "But I just received his call today," I said. "Baby, I don't know. He has been home for two days," replied Ms. Michelle. I was heated at the fact that he lied to me. My man was home for two days and he didn't call me. What's up with that? I decided to beep him to see if he would call me back, and he did. I went off on him, "What the hell is going on that you could not call me two days ago when you came home?"

Anthony responded, "You would never understand so I will not get into it with you."

"Okay!" I replied sarcastically. And then there was an awkward pause. Between the pause, I heard someone in the background. It sounded like a woman.

"Anthony where are you?" I asked.

With no hesitation, Anthony replied, "I'm with Becky."

I shouted at the top of my lungs, "WHAT?"

Anthony said, "You would never understand."

I said, "I understand that every time it is going good for us, she is always in the mix so you need to tell me what's going on Anthony."

"I can't right now, but it's not what you think."

"The hell with you and Becky" I said and I hung up.

Anthony called me back but I hung up again. I had been hurt once again with Anthony's lies with Becky. I decide to go on with my life without Anthony. I had all the money that he had made in the last seven months and I was not going to give it back. I felt that I had earned the money after all the bull he put me through. I was not going to give him the time of day. Anthony tried to call me everyday after that incident but I did not accept his calls. Surprisingly, Anthony didn't come around looking for his money at all.

The summer was ending and four weeks had past since I had been without Anthony. My girl Rosie called to see what I was up too.

"What up?" said Rosie.

"Nothing, what up with you?"

"Well, I got a call today…" and when she said that I knew it was from Anthony. Anthony knew that when he couldn't contact me he would go right my best friend Rosie.

I said, "Yes, what does he want?"

Rosie laughed and said, "What do you think he wants?"

I said, "Becky!" I said and Rosie continued to laugh.

"What is so funny?" I asked.

"Well, you're wrong," she replied.

"What he wants out of a sista'?"

"THE sista'," Rosie replied.

"Rosie, I'm tired."

"Of what?"

"You act as though it's ok for Anthony to be going back and

forth with Becky and I."

Rosie said, "There are some things that you will never know."

It was the 80's and Rosie and I were like a duet. I was responsible and Rosie was reckless. She played the dice game and knew all the street hoods, and could relate to the game. Instead, I was a woman who was the motherly type. Most guys saw me as a wifey and I did not have children, it was Rosie that had the children.

I said, "Rosie why is Anthony calling you with this stuff?"

Rosie said, "Anthony knows that I will understand and you won't so why don't you give him a call and ask him all the questions that you need answered. It is time that he tell you."

I said, "Okay, tell him to call me."

"No, I told Anthony to pick you up." Rosie was like Anthony's mediator. She helped solve all of Anthony's problems but she was my best friend.

Anthony beeped me and I called him back. He said to be ready because he was going to pick me up around ten o'clock that evening and that he would answer all of my burning questions. Anthony would have some questions for me as well when he arrived to my home to find my parents gone. At that time, I hadn't revealed to anyone, not even my best friend Rosie, that I was living on my own. One day, I returned home from work to find the apartment was empty. I picked up a note that was left on the refrigerator that read:

We love you but it's time that you become a woman and be on your own. Me and your father bought a condo in New Jersey. Here's the address:
271 Cherry Street, Newark N.J.

There was a number that they left but I was so surprised that I chose not to call at that time. For a few days, I felt abandoned but I realized it was because I was so comfortable with my life and my parents did not want me to be an old lady living with them forever so they decided to leave me. It was they best decision they made for me. I was 27 years old and it was their way to force me on my own without leaving me out on the street to fend for myself. I held no grudges. They did the right thing for me.

Anthony not calling me when he got home was like another kick in the butt. Anthony was my man and I wanted to share the good news that I was on my own but he messed that up for me. At 8:30 p.m., I began to get prepared to meet Anthony. At 10:00 p.m., the telephone rang and Anthony asked, "Where is mommy and daddy?" I told him that they were at my brother's house. He then asked me to go downstairs since he had arrived. We decided in the car that we would go to mine and Rosie's after hour breakfast spot, *Galaxy Dine.*

When we arrived to *Galaxy*, I ordered a lobster with mashed potatoes and corn, and Anthony ordered two lobsters with wild rice and some string beans. We decided not to spoil our meal with questions so we ate and then talked afterward.

I asked, "Anthony why did you not tell me you were home?"

Anthony said, "I just wanted to see if you were still faithful to me. I was gone almost a month and I know that it was not been the best when I left you."

"And about the Becky stuff?"

"There are things that you will never do and I would not want you to do for me. You are my woman and not my runner."

I said, "What do you mean?"

Anthony said, "Well Becky works sometimes for me."

"Doing what?"

"Well baby, Becky works in a place that sells guns and I get them from her."

I didn't know how to feel at that particular moment, "What?"

Anthony said, "Becky works for an army base and that's where I get them from."

I said, "What do you mean? Why you need guns?"

"I don't want you to know. You don't need to know too much just believe that it's not physical why Becky and I are together."

"I would like to go home," I replied.

Anthony asked, "Are there anymore questions?"

"No, take me home."

I knew that he was involved in some deep stuff and I did not want to know anything else. We left *Galaxy Diner* and went to my house. When I opened up the door to my apartment and Anthony walked in he said, "Mommy and Daddy redecorated the house." I looked at him and said, "My parents moved out. Anthony, that was the good news that I wanted to share with you a month ago but you didn't tell me the truth about when you got home so I just kept it to myself." Anthony asked what happened and I began to cry. I explained to him the reasoning behind the move. "Fita, why are you crying? Your parents love you. They just want you to become all that they raised you to be. Stop crying baby. It's not abandonment. Stop! Grow up."

His words encouraged me to call my parents. I hadn't spoken to them in weeks. At 1:00 a.m., I called to say hello and to tell them that I loved them. My mother picked up and asked, "You all right?"

"Yes, it's just hard getting use to being by myself."

My father got on the telephone and asked, "Where is Anthony?" I said, "He is here."

"Put him on the telephone."

Anthony said, "Hey dad!"

My father said, "Take care of my baby girl," and he hung up.

Anthony hung up the telephone and said, "Let's go to bed." I asked Anthony in bed what did my father say and Anthony replied, "Nothing I can't handle," and we went to sleep.

I slept like a baby that night. I was in my bed with a man that loved me. We were two birds in a nest. It was about 10:00 a.m., and I got up and looked at how Anthony was sleeping. He looked so peaceful. From that day, I knew that I wanted him to be with me every night. I got up and cooked breakfast. Over breakfast, Anthony said, "Your father said to take care of his baby girl and I gave him my word." Anthony got up and went to take a shower and I joined him. We of course made love in the shower, and got out and went into the living-room because Anthony wanted to talk.

"Let's start by counting some of your money," Anthony said.

"My money? I don't have a lot to count?" I replied with a frazzled face.

"You are so faithful. The money that I give you is yours."

I went to the room and took out the safe, and Anthony began counting the money. He said "If something should happen to me I want you to move from Queens." The way he looked at me, I could tell he was serious. Anthony explained to me a little more about his involvement in his "business" and we decided to split the money in piles for hard times, with lawyer and bail money fees separate.

After separating the money, I put it away and both Anthony and I began to get dressed. I was going to Rosie's house while Anthony had some things to take care of. In the meantime, his pager went off and he noticed it was one of his worker's beeping him. When he called back, he spoke with Eli who explained to him that Roe had gotten busted with a lot of drugs. Anthony asked Eli what was the bail amount was and he replied $10,000. Anthony said, "What?" I guess the conversation Anthony and I just had was important. Anthony must have known that something was going to happen soon. Anthony hung up the phone and advised me that he needed to go do something and that I should stay home.

Once Anthony left, I picked up the phone to call Rosie. The whole time I was on the phone I was mostly thinking of Anthony and if he was okay. Rosie said, "Fita, why are you not talking? What's on your mind?" I said, "Nothing. I was just thinking of my parents." I lied. My beeper vibrated and I told Rosie that would call her back. It was Anthony beeping me. When I called Anthony, he informed me that he was okay but he needed me to take him $5,000 to "The Ave." I was confused. I said, "Where?" Anthony said, "Come to White Castle on Lefferts Blvd in Queens." I immediately got in my car and headed to meet my man. I was hopeful that things were okay.

I arrived to the location and drove into the drive-through when Anthony jumped in the car and took the money, and hopped right back out. Since he didn't say anything, I figured he was all set so I went back home. At about 3:00 a.m., Anthony called me and asked that I go get him.

Anthony said, "Hey baby! How was your day?"

I said, "Anthony I did not go to Rosie 's thinking of your day."

"I'm sorry! That is why I don't tell you much. I know you worry."

I picked Anthony up and he stayed at my house another night. I was so happy to have him lye next to me. On Monday, after work, I beeped Anthony to check and see if his day went okay, and to make sure everything was alright with his business. When he called me back at home, he informed me that he was home and was okay but that he needed to go out of town one last time.

"Anthony said, "I need for you to rent a car baby. We are going out of town next weekend."

I said, "Who?"

"Not you."

"Oh! Okay."

Anthony said, "I'm going to come over tonight. Okay?"

I said, "Yes!"

When Anthony arrived, he said, "Baby, I have to go out of town for Roe to make the money back that came out of the bail money." Anthony was very serious about being short on money. He wanted to be a millionaire. He always dreamt big for us. I rented the car and he said, "Rent you one too." I asked, "Why?" "Why do you ask so many questions? Just do it." To avoid anymore conflict, I called and made reservations to pick up a car from Avis at Kennedy Airport. I rented Anthony's from a car rental place on Flatlands Ave and Pennsylvania Ave. This was a rental car place that took cash, credit cards weren't a requirement unlike Avis.

The next day, I got off of work and Anthony picked me up and we went to pick up the vehicles. At 7:30 p.m., Anthony told me he was leaving and wouldn't return for two days. Two days came and went and there was no Anthony. I beeped him and when he called, he said that the day wasn't good for him to head back home so that he would be staying until the weekend. The rest of the week, I went to work thinking of Anthony's whereabouts and if something happened. If so, how would I know where exactly he was? All I could do was pray for him.

On Friday, God sent my man home in one piece. It was always scary when Mr. Anthony wanted to open up in a new place out of town; somewhere he really didn't know many people but he had the gift to get to know them. Anthony went out of town a few more times like it was a professional job that required him to travel. He would be out of town three times a week for about two months. One day I asked Anthony, while making love, "Why did you jump out of your sleep the other morning?"

Anthony said, "I think that someone is watching me."

"Why do you feel that way?"

"It's like I see the same people when I go in and out of town."

I asked, "What do you mean?"

Anthony said, "The last time you rented that car, it seemed as though the man that has been following me was at the rental car place when we went to return the car."

"Why didn't you mention that before?"

"I did not want to worry you but you see I stoped asking you to rent cars."

As we got up out of the bed for the day, Anthony wanted to stop at his Aunt Nickie's house. Aunt Nickie lived in Atlantic Towers in Brownsville, BK. I realized that Anthony was worried about something but he did not say anything at that time. We drove to Aunt Nickie's house, and when we got on the elevator I asked Anthony what was on his mind. He said he was very nervous. He was still feeling like someone was following him so he wanted me to leave and go to Rosie's house. Rosie lived only about 15 minutes away, down on Strauss between Blake and Dumont. Before I left Aunt Nickie's, her house phone rang and because I was standing next to it, I picked it up and said hello. No one answered. The person on the other end hung up. Anthony's cousin Michael asked, "Fita, who was on the telephone? Was it my girl?" I said, "No Mike. The person hung up." The telephone rang again and I picked up and said hello again. This time, the person said, "Hello! Is Willis there?" I said, "Who?" "Willis Barbour there?" I was stuck on stupid because not too many people knew Anthony's real name so I said, "Who's calling?" The person said, "It John from Avis car rental." I went to get Anthony and when he said hello, Anthony told me there was no one on the telephone. The Phone rang again and Anthony answered it. This time when Anthony said hello, there were people knocking at the door. It was a hard knock, like ATF. At the same time that Anthony was answering the phone, Michael answered the door.

Anthony had been set up. It was the police at the door. They had tapped the telephones in the building to make sure that he was at his aunt's house. Anthony never kept anything in my house or his house but he would keep his guns at Aunt Nickie's. Anthony jumped out onto the apartment terrace. He jumped from one terrace to another. He finally went into someone's house who had their terrace door open and jumped into the shower but the police followed him into the tenant's bathroom.

When the police got back to Aunt Nickie's house, they said that they were Federal Police Agents and they had been following Anthony for months but they did not want him for the drugs, it was for the guns (those freaking guns, the ones that the witch Becky had given him). She turned federal evidence in on him. The Feds found out about the $5,000 and the three guns that were missing from the military base. They took Anthony and Michael, and left me. I did not understand what happened but I am sure glad that God had my back. The Feds also had Becky at Federal Plaza waiting to point Anthony out as the theft. I called Aunt Nickie to let her know and she was nervous because Aunt Nickie was a transit worker. She did not want the Feds to know how Anthony was related to her and why the guns were in her house. She thought she was going to lose her job.

At Federal Plaza, Anthony stood up and said, "I will take all the charges. Don't get my aunt or my cousin involved. Thank you for not arresting my girl. They have nothing to do with it. This is something they are not involved in. Please let them go." In the meantime, I called Ms. Michelle and told her what had happen and she said angrily, "I told the boy to stop dealing with Becky. She did not mean him any good. Where are you?" I told her we were at Federal Plaza, downtown.

I did not know what to do so I just cried and cried, and stayed with Aunt Nickie. She said, "I did not know that him and Michelle had those guns in my house. Where did that boy get those guns from?"

"Becky," I replied sarcastically.

"I told him to stop dealing with that girl; to just stay with you. I told that boy don't bring that girl in my house."

"He brought her to your house?"

"What? You act like you don't know?"

I said, "What?"

Nickie said, "She and Anthony always meet in my house because Michelle does not want Becky at her house."

"What!"

"I love my nephew and he is my favorite but I don't like that you are so true and he is still playing around. I told him he needs to stay with one woman."

The whole situation was crazy. There I was with that man and I didn't know that he was still with Becky. He had told me something different and I believed him. I decided that that would be the end of Anthony feeding me his bull. I wanted to go on with my life. I was getting ready to start a new job and it was around a lot of other men. Maybe God placed me there to find a good man. Anthony knew that I was tired of the life that he had me living and he was forcing me into leaving his butt for good. The back and forth with Ms. Becky, I was so over it.

I went on home trying to forget what happened but it was on my mind so bad that I had to talk to someone. I couldn't talk to my parents because they would have said, "I told you that would happen because of the direction that you were going." Instead, I decided to call Rosie and cry. I explained everything to Rosie and she said, "Why don't you come to my house. You should not be alone." When I arrived, she opened the door and I said "What the hell?" questioning why this stuff always happened to me. Rosie said, "Don't sweat it. You will be fine. What you need to do is just go on with your life. You are going to meet new people so just take it like a champ."

The next day, I woke up alone with no Anthony by my side. As I got ready for work, the phone rang and it was Anthony. "I'm sorry," he said. I said, "Okay, just try to get yourself together." I decided not to mention everything that his aunt had said to me. It wasn't worth it. Anthony was now facing some real time and there was no reason to argue about Becky. Anthony said he would call once he got to where he was going to be officially placed. I said yeah and began to cry. I went off to work and began to take one day at a time.

Chapter IX

Alone

Anthony had been away for a few weeks now. He was being held at the Metropolitan Correctional Center (MCC) in NYC, located on Chamber Street. I had been to see him a few times but it was very difficult seeing him that way. I was also getting tired of doing the prison bid thing again. Ms. Becky had turned federal evidence on him so she could not go to see him. Instead, I took on the deed to go at least once a week to see him until he was sent to Otisville Federal Correctional Facility in Orange County, New York.

A few months past since Anthony got locked up. I was so engulfed in what had happened to him, I almost forgot about my own life. I found myself playing catch up. It's a rough road trying to work and visit your man in prison. Between visiting, putting money in his account, and sending him clothes and food packages, I could never get myself together. By the time I realized it was another summer.

It was now July and Anthony had been locked up for about seven months. At the end of the month, I was going to start a new job. I was scheduled to begin on July 30, 1990 after resigning from the Department of Education. On July 29th, I was scheduled to be in a wedding. It was weird for me. The fact that I was going to be around a bunch of people in love and the man that I loved was in a federal penitentiary. It was very hard going down the aisle as a bride's maid. This was after being asked to be the Maid of Honor for my first cousin Clarissa's wedding one year prior. With all the weddings that I had helped to plan and had been in, I felt as though my chance to marry was gone now.

I needed to get over myself and get my positive attitude back for my big day. I needed to make sure I focused on the new opportunity

God had provided to me. With everything happening in my life, I failed to realize that I was doing a great thing working for sanitation. I was going to be one of the first women to work for the NYC Department of Sanitation. It slipped my mind after missing the department's formal celebration for women because I was so involved with Anthony's court dates and his prison move. I realize how much of a pioneer and legend I was going to be along with my fellow women cohorts. I was a part of a big movement for the department. I made history.

At the time, there were about 7,500 men working for the department and I was chosen to be one of the women on the team. When I got called, I was number twenty on the list, meaning there were only nineteen women called before me. That was an honor.

Anthony was never insecure of men in my presence. He was secure that I would not cheat on him. I celebrated my success with Anthony at my next visit to MCC. Rosie and I also went out to celebrate my new job. It was the first time in a long time that we had so much fun. I could feel that things were going to get better for me. I thought that by me taking the job, Anthony would stop hustling. But instead, Anthony was incarcerated in the federal prison and didn't have a chance to do that. Instead, he got locked up.

Sanitation was a good job and I would make so much more money. I felt at ease. Working School Safety allowed me to meet a lot of police officers. I feared that one day I would encounter a police officer that I knew as a result of my man's wrong doings. I felt safer in my new environment. I was now driving truck and picking up NYC garbage. It wasn't as bad as it sounds.

This job seemed so much different then any other job I ever had. The men at my garage were crazy and funny, and both young and old. The experience was different for everyone, especially since the men weren't use to a woman at the garage. At BKN3 Garage, there were about 14 women and 175 men. The beginning of my career with the department was when Anthony was locked up. He would to call my job so that the men knew I wasn't single. At the same time, he didn't want my co-workers to think anything was up with him, especially since no one knew he was locked up.

As time went on and I went back and forth to court, the prosecutor was trying to offer Anthony 20 years for the three guns. Not once was he prosecuted for all the drug operations and drug sales. They really wanted him for the guns. I was sick when I heard 20 years. I got a sighting of me being old, waiting for my man. Anthony' lawyer , at the time, Mr. Elephant got the charge reversed to 3 to 6 years instead. At the court, God was with us. I could breathe now. Now, I would have an opportunity to share some real time with my man and have a life after all this bull. After the trial, I went to see Anthony one more time before he was sent to Otisville Correctional.

At work, I was on training with another man who was showing me "the ropes." There was no driving involved until I received my Classes B License. In the early 90's, a person could be accepted into the job without a Class B but you would have to get the license within the training period, otherwise you would be terminated. Training was only for two weeks.

The image that I portrayed to my co-workers was one that was very exclusive. The men in my garage knew that my love affair with Mr. Anthony was special. Not for a moment did I ever have anyone know that Anthony worked out on the street. I had so many people fooled that we were inseparable but little did they know that I was alone in this love affair because my other half was in the prison. It was like living in a fantasy world the first year on my new job. However, I managed to keep a smile and I stayed busy.

During the holidays, which were right around the corner, I got very sensitive. It was always hard for me. All of my loved ones would get together and I would join them, minus Anthony. November came and the eating of turkey arrived but I was eating alone. Although I went to my family's house, I had no man and I felt detached. Christmas time came and the exchanging of gifts came and went. At my age, it was best to exchange gifts with a mate but I didn't have mine present. New Year's was a time when most women would love to be in the presence of their man making love when the ball dropped, but again my man wasn't around to spend these times with. And then my least favorite holiday, for a while, was Valentines Day; the day for lovers. This day made me sick to my stomach; just looking at all the people that where in love. I always felt awful. I hated going to the store and having everything surrounding me be chocolate hearts, long stemmed red roses, and jewelry. I also hated to watch television because of the stupid Pocono Resort commercial that played fifty times a day with a couple enjoying wine in a hot tub shaped like a champagne glass. I was disgusted. All the things that I had wanted and deserved, I was deprived of because of my foolish man deciding to deal with that witch Becky and now he is locked up doing three to six. I was so upset at him.

The first few years were hard on me but it got a little better. As time went on, I began to get accustomed to the situation. With a switch in my shift at work, I would barely have time to see Anthony and he started to get mad. As a result, we argued a lot. I was about 16 months into my job and I decided to treat myself by buying a smoke grey four door 1990 Audi 5000. It was my first foreign car.

I was working so hard and doing such great things but I had no one to share these things with. I began putting in a lot of time with my female co-workers by going to the gym and working out. I also participated in the woman's association within the department. For some reason, people saw me as a revolutionary. I was not to be played with. Through my involvement with the association, I made a name for myself. I had a strong voice.

In the mist of my professional success, I later felt that I had been denying my man the attention he needed. Although we spoke everyday, I hadn't seen Anthony in three months. Anthony was not really worried about me cheating; he wanted to hear everything that was going on in my life. I guess he wanted me to paint some type of picture in his brain to keep him smiling. But all his questions started to annoy me. Some made me feel as if I had to ask him permission to enjoy myself. Our conversations escalated and we had a big argument about not visiting as much as he felt I should. We decided to just let this go and I said, "Mr. Anthony I think you need to see someone else because this is not for me. I did not put you in here so I don't have to take this crap." Anthony apologized and of course I forgave him. We kissed and joked around with each other.

Following the visit, I made it my business to visit him more. We discussed our plans for when he returned home. I went to see Anthony on a surprise visit once but I was the one surprised. That stupid fool was on a visit with that slut Becky. This was too far of a trip to play games so I got right on the visit and I said, "Anthony, I have had enough," and I walked out. I was so done. I never wanted him to find me again.

It was about a three hour drive home, and I began to put my feelings aside. I needed to deal with this head up. I decided that I needed to stop making excuses for Anthony's stupidity. I needed to begin changing my life and putting Anthony out of it. I started by changing my telephone number. That was my first step of really leaving Mr. Anthony. There couldn't be any phone contact. I went to bed feeling like tomorrow was a new beginning.

I woke up and called Rosie. She asked what the heck happened to my telephone number. It wasn't showing up on her caller ID. I said, "I changed my number."

Rosie said, "Oh boy! What's up?" I told her what happened and she said, "You are on that again?" I said, "I'm not dealing with him anymore. That's why I changed my number. I will call you back I have to my parents and brother to give them the new number."

I called my parents and brother, and told them I changed the number because I was getting to many prank calls. I called a couple of my friends and gave them the number as well. The next day, my girlfriend Michelle beeped me while I was at work. She was one of my students when I worked at George Westinghouse High School. I called her back and gave her my new number. She and I spoke briefly. She mentioned she was living in Staten Island. I told her I'd call her later because I was still on the job.

After work, I got to the garage and took a shower. While I was getting dressed in the locker room, my beeper went off. It was my cousin Tata. When I called her back, she asked about the house phone as well. She had been trying to call me the night before. I apologized and gave her the new number. My beeper went off all day. People were trying to find out what happened to me because they couldn't get through on the old number. I just called each of them back and gave them my new contact info.

As the days went on, things began to get easier for me. Except one day, I got home and there was a letter from Anthony. I did not want to open it but while my mind said no my heart said yes. I was fighting my feelings and my heart won. As I read the letter, I cried but I still had to be a "tuff guy."

A year went by, and I did not write back. I was serious about leaving him. I kept reading the letters he had sent until I couldn't read anymore. The begging, the sorry's, and the I love you's made it hard for me to stay tuff so I had to ignore them.

"Happy New Year," it was January 1991. I'm a sucker. I decided to write Anthony for the New Year. It had been six months since him and I had contact. I had been thinking of moving out of my apartment. I wanted to buy a house. I had promised my friend Michelle that I would go out to see her in Staten Island but I could never get out there. However, one day I was talking to Michelle about looking for a house and she said, "You should come out to Shaolin a.k.a. Staten Island. I said, "Girl that's too far and besides I don't think that I have the time to look for a house." My job was so demanding during the winter months that I couldn't make plans because I was on call. Instead, I asked Michelle to look for me.

Michelle was no joke. Before I knew it, I was closing on my first house in Shaolin. God had allow me to purchase a two family home with a drive way and a big backyard. It was at 192 Victory Blvd. It was big and beautiful. Both levels had two bedrooms and enough space for my family to stay and visit whenever they wanted. I was so impress with Myself. I called my parents right away and told them the good news. I said, "It's time that we get back together." And my parents agreed. On February 19, 1991 I moved in. I was glad to be with my parents again. They sold their condo and moved in downstairs.

Chapter X

Living in Shaolin

February 19, 1991, was a cold and blustery day. It began to snow as my family and I moved into our new house on Staten Island. The house was a bit old, but it was big and it was mine. The house still had its original gas fixture from the early 1900's, like from the ones you would see in old black and white films. Some had even told me that the house was used for Madonna's "Like a Virgin" video. It was the scene where she is walking down the front steps, onto the sidewalk. I haven't seen the video in so long to confirm.

The house was located near the corner of Westervelt Ave and Victory Blvd. We were conveniently near a 24 hour gas station/mini-mart where my family and I would stop in to purchase small items. Across the street was a real-estate agency and diagonally on the other side was a six family building that housed many families with children. I would later observe the kids playing outside during the summer while their parents/grandparents sat out playing cards and dominoes, while drinking a cold beer.

Aside from the snow, my parents and I were very excited to be moving into the house. We had been separated for about one year. In a year, I had endured a lot of stuff. I was excited to have my parents around to console and rescue me from my nightmares. They were my true best friends. It took me awhile, but I learned that parents know more then we think they do.

The house was upstairs/downstairs. I chose to live upstairs to avoid my parents having to go up and down each day at their old age. My parents began to pick out paint colors and decorations for their apartment and I did the same for mine. My mother Hilda and I looked through a number of magazines to get an idea of different decorations for the house. However, I was mostly the one looking. My mom had already set-up her scenery in her mind. It took about three months before us McEachin's were satisfied with our look. We defiantly shopped until we dropped.

I started out commuting from Staten Island to Brooklyn for work. Traveling back and forth became a pain, so I put in a transfer to work on Staten Island but of course there was a waiting list. One night after work when I got home, my dad asked, "Baby, what's up with all this change? First, it was your number and now the address. And you have not mentioned Anthony once."

I said, "A girl got to do what a girl got to do."

My dad Buddy (nickname) said, "Okay! What happened? Why is he incarcerated?"

"He will always be the man that I love, but I have to move on," I replied as I began to cry.

I began explaining everything that had happened in Atlantic Towers and how I thought Anthony was only seeing me but instead he was still dealing with Becky. She turned Anthony into the Feds for the guns. I mentioned to my dad that I wanted to start a totally fresh life. My father asked, "What about Anthony?" I said, "What about him?" "You could change your telephone number and you could change your address but how about your heart? That's something that you can't change so you did all this for what?" At that time in my life, it was as empty as someone drinking soda and leaving the empty can behind. I could not change my heart. From that day on, I realized that it didn't matter where you go if you can't change your heart then you will just be in a new location with the same feelings.

After a long talk with my father, things always were clearer. This is what I was missing when my parents moved and left me in Queens. This was a new beginning for me to try and resolve my feelings for Mr. Anthony. I decided to write Anthony and see how he was doing. I really wanted to see how he felt about the decision I had made for us. I figured that I would go and see him once a month before he was going to be sent to Indiana to a federal correctional facility. It took Anthony some time to write me back being that he had to get over the way I vanished. As I waited for Anthony to write me back, I started to keep myself occupied with my friends.

During the waiting process, I started to go out more with my best friend Rosie. Her kids Jhameek and Jhanee were bigger and her mother Jackie would watch them. It was fun to hang out like old times.

One night, Rosie and I went to the Empire Skating Rink that's in Brooklyn. There, I met two guys, Kenny and Marquis. Marquis was a cute light skinned brother that had approached me when I exited the skating floor. He had been watching me skate and tried kicking it to me. I stopped to give him some conversation when he mentioned that he had lived in Staten Island. I told him I did as well. He then introduced me to his friend Kenny who also lived in Staten Island. After disclosing their address, we realized that we lived right around the corner from each other. Later, I would become good friends with them and even Kenny's girlfriend Wanda.

Wanda and I started hanging out once Kenny introduced her to me when we got back to Shaolin. Wanda knew everyone on the Island. She was from West Brighten and I lived in New Brighten. We later became a team. She introduced me to lots of people and we had tons of fun.

One evening, I asked my girls from Brooklyn to visit me on the Island to hang out. Rosie, Gwen, Linda, Anita and myself went to a big party on the Island and represented BK. The party was at club *Consequences* on Bay Street also known as the "Babysitters" club to my mom.

She always made fun of the club because it had nothing but a young crowd to her.

At the club, I noticed a guy looking at me. He was a fine brown skinned guy with black wavy hair and side-burns that connected to his beard. His eye-brows were bushy and had lips to die for. The brother was about 5'7" and weighed about 175 pounds, and was bowlegged like I like them'. The handsome guy kept looking at me so I pointed to him and asked Wanda if she knew him.

Wanda said, "Oh! His name is Junie."

Then Rosie came over to me and said, "What up with that brother looking at you?"

I said, "I don't know him but he is fine." Rosie said, "Yes he is, so what's up?" "Nothing," I replied. By now, all of my BK girls had come over to where I was and noticed the same thing. I became a little frightened but I figured it wouldn't hurt to get to know him. "Wanda so what's up?" I asked. I wanted her to introduce me but when all of us looked up, he was gone.

The girls and I partied until 2:30 a.m. before most of the girls wanted to leave. Afterward, we went to eat breakfast at *Perkins* on Foster Ave. We ate and then Gwen drove the girls back to Brooklyn and I went on home.

The next afternoon, I called Wanda to shoot the breeze about the party the night before and of course asked about Junie. Wanda said, "He be on Jersey Street." I said, "Well!" Wanda said, "Well! What is that, a sign that you want to meet him?" "Yeah but I can't get serious with him but I do need a friend." "I will introduce you but Kenny does not get along with him." "I don't care about Kenny, that's your man. I'm not out to please Kenny, you are," I replied. For the next few days, I saw Junie but we had not been introduced so I just kept driving by him while he was chilling outside.

By that time, Wanda had moved in around the corner with her man Kenny so I was at her house a lot more. The weather was getting warmer and she and I began hanging out with a bunch of girls from the Island. I was having a great time getting to know the in's and out's of Shaolin. One day, I decided to walk to Jersey Street to the Chinese restaurant to get chicken wings and french fries. While at the store, I bumped into Kenny's sister Tasha. She said, "Fita there is a guy that has been wanting to meet you. He said he watches you drive by him everyday." I said, "Tasha who is this guy?" Tasha replied, "Just come with me across the street." I said okay and we crossed. When I realized, it sure enough was Junie. "Fita this is Junie," said Tasha. I said hello and Junie said the same. He asked how I was doing and I said I was doing fine. I asked him the same and he replied, "I'm alright now that I met you." I smiled but found his line to be corny. Junie continued to say, "I have been noticing you on The Ave." I asked, "What Ave?" He said, "That's what we call Jersey St." "Well that's the only way I know how to get to my friend's house." "You don't have to explain that to me. I enjoy looking at you." I said, "Okay... Well, I have to get the food that I ordered from the Chinese restaurant." Junie said, "Okay, but promise me that you will come see me on The Ave." "I will try. I can't promise you." "Fair enough." After I picked up my food, I ate and went to Wanda's house; there I was smiling all day just thinking of where things could go with Junie. However, I still thought of Anthony and him not responding back to my letters.

During the week of my birthday, I drove home on the Verrazano bridge and my beeper started to vibrate. It was number an unfamiliar number. Once I got home, I called the number back and it was a guy. "Hello!" I said. The male voice replied, "Hey! How are you?" "Okay" As we continued to speak, the voice became more familiar. "Junie?" He said, "Yes!" I asked, "How did you get my number." Junie replied, "I got it from Tasha. Is that a problem?" "No but why didn't you ask me for my number." "I didn't want you to know that I was sweating you so I asked Tasha for the number yesterday." I said, "Why did you ask for my number?" Junie said, "I know from our conversation that you have a birthday coming this month and I wanted to take you out or do something for you." "Junie I appreciate that but I'm not your average girl. I am very expensive." "I can see that. You drive a 1992 Audi 5000" I laughed and said, "I drink Alize and Moet." Junie laughed and said, "Well, now that you got that out of the way, would you like to go out with me on your birthday?" "Well I need to tell you that I have a man." Junie said, "Okay are we on for our day of adventure?" I said, "Yes! I will be off of work on my birthday and I will come straight home and I will beep you." "Okay, but today is open for me. Would you like to go to the park and talk?" "Sure. I need about an hour and I will meet you at Wanda's house on Westervelt Ave." "I don't talk with her people so I will meet you on The Ave." I said, "Okay."

It had been a long time since I been out on a date with someone. I was excited and nervous. I had been out of the dating scene for more than four years, not to say that I was not sharp when I was dating my man, but this was a new person and things were different. Nonetheless, I got all cute and I went to The Ave.

As I pulled up in my car, Junie was on the corner with some of his peoples and when he noticed me he smiled. Junie had a beautiful smile, with pretty white teeth just like Anthony. Junie said, "Hey! You look nice." I said, "Thank you!" "Lets walk to the park." "Why?" Junie said, "I want to see you walk and talk or is that belittling your standers." "No, I will walk." "So tell me about yourself." I said, "What do you want to know?" "For starters, what is your race? Where are you from? And what about your man?" I said, "Well, I'm half Black American and Puerto Rican. I was born in Brooklyn. I lived in Brooklyn until I was 17 years old and then moved to Queens. My man is away." Junie said, "Away where? In prison?" I said, "Yes." Junie then said, "Where does that lead us?" "Well I don't know but I do know that I am in love with my man." "So is there any room for me?" "I would like to start off as friends." Junie looked at me an said, "Okay, fair enough. So would you like to go out from time to time?" "Yes, it would be nice." Then I reversed the questions on Junie. "What's your race? Where are you from? And what about the girl in your life?" Junie answered, "Well, I have Black American, Hondurian and Indian blood. I was born on Staten Island and I don't have a girlfriend but I do have a set of twin boys." I was overwhelmed by his remark. I had a lose for words; not that he had sons but this brother was a twin maker. I asked Junie, "So what are your twins' names?" Junie responded, "Tayquan and Equan." "What happened with the boys' mother?" "Nothing, we are not together...we were never together. It was that her parents were not there for her and my mother took her in and I was a boy and she was a girl and we played house and she got pregnant." Shocking! Here I was talking to a very nice man that didn't appear to be nice. Everyone on

Shaolin had a very bad taste for Junie but he was revealing to me so much more.

At about 10:00 p.m., we walked to The Ave back from the park. It was getting late and I needed to get home. While I was entering my car, Junie said, "I enjoyed you Fita." I said, "I enjoyed you too Junie." Then I got in my car and drove to me house about three blocks away. That night, I thought of Junie and his life. I said to myself thank you God for keeping me focus.

It was the day before my birthday and I was going to work. I had been talking to Junie the whole week and was excited to go out with him for my birthday. For a moment, I actually started to forget about Anthony. I was starting to get use to Junie as my partner. I was happy to once again get on with my life. After work, I went straight to my house. For the past four months, I would go home to find my mailbox empty, no response from Anthony. But when I checked this particular day, there letter from Anthony (the day before my birthday). What a gift. It said Happy Birthday My Love! As I read the letter, it brought back so many memories. I stood reading it over and over again. Anthony really knew how to lay it down in his letters so that I would always think of him before I made a mistake in my life. But it was too far of a wait so I decided to go on with my life. I made up my mind and was going out with Junie. This was the day I had been waiting for but I could not concern myself with what was on that letter because Anthony was not home and I was going out on my date. Junie arrived to my house to pick me up. I had told my parents that I was going out with a friend even though my parents didn't concern themselves with who was ringing the doorbell. They understood that I was trying to go on with my life. As I walk downstairs to the door, my father asked if I was going to be aright and I said yes.

Junie took me to eat at this restaurant on Foster Ave on Staten Island. Junie and I had such a good time and were inseparable. Junie had put some fun into my life. Junie said, "You have to come with me. I have something to give you for your birthday." We walked to another part of the restaurant and it was lit with candles and a bottle of Moet and Alize was laid out on one of the tables. It was very unexpected so I began to cry. Tears of joy left my eyes as we exited the restaurant the staff said Happy Birthday. For the first time, I looked at Junie and said thank you and I kissed him. Junie still had reminded me of Anthony, the way he walked, talked, and put me first. I continued to write Anthony to see if we could rebuild our relationship. But I was still spending a lot of time with Junie we were building our relationship. I went through the spring and summer months with Junie, and I was still writing Anthony. I had two men in my life. Junie knew of Anthony but Anthony did not know about Junie. The summer was over and I knew that Anthony would be transferring back to the NYC from Indiana. Anthony had done six months in Indiana Federal Correction and it was time for him be back MCC. I had spoken to Junie about what was going on with my man and he just played it by ear. But on the other hand, I was bonding with Junie even though we didn't have sex. Yet we rubbed, bumped, and humped as we kissed each night. The cold weather was on its way, and I still was working in Brooklyn. I had not yet got my transfer to Staten Island. I was going into my second year with sanitation, and my third winter with the department. As the holidays rolled around, I prepared to spent time with my new man Junie. I wasn't actually going to be with him and his family but at least I knew I had someone that was accessible unlike Anthony. I spent Thanksgiving in the Bronx with my parents because it was my Junior and his wife's year to cook. I was able to spend quality time with my two nieces Victoria and Stephanie, and Chino my nephew. I always had a good time with my family. I would always sing and my nieces and nephew thought that I was a star. I loved playing with the kids since we didn't spend much time together because we lived so far away from each other. Therefore, when we spent time together we enjoyed every minute of it. On the other hand, Junie was kind of upset that he had not met my family yet. We had been seeing each other for about four months but my family was sacred to me. Introducing him or any other person in my life to my family had to be earned. Thanksgiving came and went, and it was now Christmas. I had spoken to my parents and told them that I would like to spend Christmas with Junie. I decided not to go to the Bronx so I asked my parents to take the gifts. They were just fine with my decision and took my car to drive up to the Bronx. When they left, I immediately dressed to give Junie a special Christmas and a special gift. For six months, I had committed myself to Junie. I don't know what I was going to tell Anthony but I was ready to be true to Junie and only Junie.

Nevertheless, after I dressed I cooked a special meal for my man. I made baked macaroni and cheese, turkey, and ham . I set the table for two with candies a bottle of Alize. I told Junie that I would have dinner ready at 7:00 p.m. Exactly at 7:00 p.m. the doorbell rang. I went to the door with my hair in shirley temple curls and a long red robe with black Fredricks flip flop mick-heels. I just swung the door open and turned around to have Junie look at me strut my stuff. When I untied my robe, Junie had an astonished look on his face. I had a Santa Claus teddy. What Junie did not know was that the teddy was eatable. As I took his Nautica Goose off, Junie was shocked. I said, "Baby, lets go to get the dinner that I prepared for us." Junie followed me into the kitchen and watched as I fixed dinner. At the dinner table Junie said, "I have never had a girl do this for me." I replied, "I'm not a girl. You have a young woman on your hands now." Junie then blew out the candles and it was over.

I had underestimated Junie. He had a lot in his pants and he knew how to work it (God had definitely blessed him). This was the beginning of my love affair with Junie. We had sex all night long; there was no ending. We drank the Alize and enjoyed our Christmas together. Junie stayed at my place for about two days and then left to take care of his business. It seemed like all the men I attracted were unlicensed street pharmacist. A few days before the New Year, Junie wanted to spend time with me but I told him that I would be with my family; it was tradition. Junies understood but I noticed that he was still upset. I told Junie that after the New Year I would introduce him to my family, which excited him.

In the meantime, Junie and I had a good time discussing our first Christmas together. Junie was still shocked about how I put it on him and I was surprised at what was in his pants. We kissed that particular day and I told him I would see him on New Years. I left and went to my house to prepare for the drive to the Bronx.

As my parents and I arrived to the Bronx, I was in good sprits because I had a wonderful Christmas with my new man and I had been feeling fine. I finally released all the stored frustration that I had been having due to the lack of sex in my life; I was glowing. The first thing that was said to me as I walked in the door of my brother Junior's house was "Titi (auntie in Spanish), why did you not come for Christmas?" My oldest niece Victoria immediately questioned my absence. I said, "Well, Titi Fita had went out for Christmas." "Okay Titi, I will accept that." My niece Victoria was the oldest and she was like an old woman in a little girl's body. She was smart and was just like me when I was her age.

Later, I had the third degree from my brother and my sister-in-law but it was different. I could talk to my sister-in-law. Vickie said, "Okay Sis, tell me the real deal." I said, "Well Vickie, I wanted to spend Christmas with my new man." "What?" "Sis, I have a new man. His name is Junie." Vickie said, "What up with Anthony?" I replied, "He did not answer me about what we were going to do so I just went on with my life." As it got closer to the New Year, my family and I just talked and partied until the ball dropped. In the background, my mother Hilda walked around with her plate of spiritual incents and blessed our home. When the ball dropped, we all yelled, "HAPPY NEW YEAR!"

and hugged and kissed each other followed by more dancing and drinking.

It was January 1, 1992, and Anthony had been in prison with a release this year. But I couldn't concern myself with him coming home because I was involved with Junie, and things were going good. For the New Year, I introduced Junie to my family and by February we were living together. I got really sick and I beeped Junie while he was on The Ave, and told him that I needed him to take me to the hospital because I couldn't stop throwing up. Junie panicked and was home in 2 minutes and we headed directly to the emergency room. Upon checking into the hospital, both Junie and I were required to show photo ID. I was the patient and he was the person enrolling me into the hospital. Therefore, we needed to show proof of who we were. In the mist of being engulfed in the craziness of the hospital setting, Junie had to go to the nurse's station to complete some forms as I was being taken to a bed. One of the attendants handed me back both ID's. I had never seen Junie's photo ID so I was curious to check out his picture. When I looked, I was appalled. Junie was only 17 years old. He lied just like Anthony. He told me he was 21 when we met.

"This can't be happening to me again," I said to myself. Not only was my man a minor but I found out I was 5 weeks pregnant. That meant I got pregnant on my first encounter with Junie. We made a baby on Christmas. I was happy yet sad and Junie was excited and wanted to let my parents know. I didn't want to tell them anything because they knew that I was still in love with Anthony and I didn't want to disappoint them. But I was not getting any younger. I was 28 years old so it was time for me to be a mother. Therefore, I decided to let my parents know on Valentine's Day. I wanted to surprise them but I was the one surprised. At 9:00 p.m., Junie entered the house and I said, "Baby, lets go downstairs to my parents house and tell them about the baby." Junie said, "Okay, but let me take a shower and get dressed first," so I waited for him. When we got downstairs, my parents had a packed house. Wanda was there and a few more people that I hung-out with on Staten Island. Rosie was also there. I said, "Why are all these people here mom and dad?" My parents looked a Junie and my mom said, "Well, Junie brought all these people together so ask him." I turned to Junie and he pulled out a box of chocolate candy and said to my father, "Could I have your daughter's hand in marriage?" I laughed because it was a chocolate candy box and my father said yes. Junie looked at me and dropped to his knee and said, "Would you accept this ring in marriage?" I opened the chocolate box and it was a two carat marquis diamond ring inside of it. I cried and said, "YES!" I decided not to mention the pregnancy and instead I decided to go out with my girls. Junie said, "Baby, if you are going out remember that you are officially spoken for." I just shook my head and got ready to go out. That night, Rosie and Wanda decided to go to club *Jonzie* on Staten Island. Thursdays was crab night.

Where I lived, *Jonzie* was on the other side of the Island, off of the Terrence and South Ave near the harbor. *Jonzie's* was the joint on Thursday nights. It was buy a drink and get free crabs, but I couldn't drink so I ate all of the crabs when my girls ordered drinks. While I was seated at the bar, Rosie said, "Oh girl, you have gotten the boy to commit himself to you and what are you going to do about Anthony? You know that he will be home in July." I said "Rosi, I will climb that wall when it comes so just let me enjoy myself tonight please." Rosie said, "You're right, I'm sorry. You deserve that ring girl." As we danced and enjoyed the night, I grew tried and I had to work the next morning so I asked the girls if we could leave. I offered Rosie my guest room and told her I would take her home on my way to work. I got in the bed and about 30 minutes later my man entered the sheets and started to play with is coochie until he got what he wanted. In the morning, I went to the guest room to make sure Rosie was ready for the drive to Brooklyn. She was already dressed and was waiting for me to head out. After dropping her off home, I was excited for the day. I had just gotten engaged the night before and it would be a surprise to everyone at my job. I was feeling good about the big rock that I had on my finger. I could see all the girls at the job hating on the size and the guys questioning whether or not I'm ready to get hitched. As I walked into the garage, I just happened to touch my face with my ring finger and one of my co-workers looked and asked, "McEachin, did you get engaged for Valentine's Day?" I said, "YES!" I didn't expect a diamond that big but that's what the Lord granted me when he brought me Junie. The men at my garage were very surprised that I had gotten engaged because they were always saying that I was a pimpette and that I was too smooth to be tied down. Like I said, they didn't think I would ever get hitched. When my partner heard that I had gotten engaged he said "Pimping ain't easy." I just smiled and went into the office. When I walked into the office, I had to set up my board (it was the route that we're going to be servicing the next day for pick up). After I had done all of my office duties, I had time to think about Anthony more and more so I needed to find a solution about my decision. It was time for me to give myself some time to think of what and how I was going to tell Anthony about the pregnancy. I knew that it would upset him but I had to tell him so that I could avoid any bad vibes between us.

The week went by and I got sicker and sicker about my situation. I wish I was able to go to the Rockaways like old times and tell Anthony face-to-face but that wasn't an option anymore. I started to also think twice about my decision to marry and have a child by Junie. February ran out of the calendar and March snuck up on me. I tried having fun with my man who enjoyed my maternity. By this time, I had already told my parents that I was pregnant and it was left up to me to let Anthony know. I was an adult and I had to stand behind my decision. One day, Anthony finally called the house because he had got the number from my Rosie. The telephone rang and the operator asked if I would like to accept a collect call from a correctional facility, "Press one if you will accept and press two if you are not accepting this call." Of course I pressed one and I said "Hello...Hello!" Anthony said, "Hello Ms. McEachin, how are you doing? What is happening in your life? How many men are trying to get with you? What is with the change of address?" He had so many questions. I began with, "Anthony, I'm doing fine. The change of address came from me trying to change my life after the stuff you did before you got locked up. I spoke to your Aunt Nickie and she said you were still seeing Ms. Becky but you had me thinking differently. Anthony as far as men trying to get with me, there were a few but I didn't give them the time of day in the beginning." Anthony said, "Well then, what is the end result." "I have a friend and his name is Junie. He's a really nice guy. I told him about you and he knows that I have a man. Anthony even when you and I were not speaking, I told him about you being my man." Anthony replied, "Is that suppose to make me feel any different while you are messing around." I said, "I don't know how you feel but for once in my life I am happy." "Well, you have your fun. Just keep it real. Talk to Tom, Dick, Bill, Bob and Harry but don't just talk to Junie because that's how a relationship starts. And don't give up my stuff." I replied, "Okay!" since I didn't want to get into an argument with him. We continued to talk and laugh. Anthony always made me laugh and as I was on the telephone, Junie came in the house and asked me who I was on the phone with smiling like that, I said it was Anthony. Junie stared at me but knew all the time that this day would come so he handled it well. Anthony and I stayed on the phone for about another hour when Anthony said, "Okay baby, I have to go. I'll speak to you tomorrow. After I hung up, I took a shower and put on my pj's because it was nine o'clock and I was in for the night. When I got in the bed, Junie asked, "So what was the conversation about?" I said, "Just casual talk. We have not spoken to each other in about three months." Junie said so when are you going to tell him that he is out?" "Baby, don't start. I will handle that. "Fita, it is not that simple. It's not easy for me to accept you speaking to your other man. Know that you accepted my hand in marriage and that you are expecting my baby." I said, "Junie, lets not talk about it." "Well, if you don't tell him soon, I will get on the telephone and break it down to him and he will just have to see me." I said, "Junie, you knew that I had a man but it did not stop you from getting with me so don't get crazy now." "Well, I'm going to let you handle the situation but if you don't tell him by May, I will." Junie was giving me two months to break the news to Anthony. As I laid in bed, Junie got out of the shower and hopped into bed. As we talked more about the situation, we played with each other and made love.

It was the beginning of March and there were so many things going on in my life. I was engaged, pregnant, stressed, and in love with two men. To put the frosting on the cake, my father had gotten very sick with high blood pressure and seizures causing him to have his first stroke. I was going back and forth with my mother to the hospital. My father was at St. Vincent Hospital on Castleton Ave in Staten Island. Every night, I found myself speaking to my man Anthony and sleeping with my future husband Junie. What was I going to do? I had a short time to fix all of my chaos. Anthony was coming home this year so I had to get to it quick fast. But there was something about Anthony that allowed him to have his way with me but I had to put a stop to it. I don't know what I was in love with the most - the money, sex, excitement or that he was just my first very love. I needed my father consent to move on but he was sick. I could not talk to my mother Hilda because she was hot headed. She wouldn't understand but my father would, I was his little girl. The weeks went by slowly. My father got better and was discharged (one of my problems was cleared). I'm grateful that God answered my prayers. It was time to fix the rest of my life. As I was talking to Anthony every night and informed him that my father was home he said, "Go take care of daddy Fita because he is a good father." Then Anthony he had mentioned that he wanted to talk to Junie. I told him he wasn't home. Anthony replied, "When he gets home I want to speak to him." I asked, "For what?" "That's what men do. I respect him for taking care of my woman." It was time to change the subject because Anthony was getting to deep for me and I was not in the right frame of mind. Anthony and I spoke for a little while longer and Junie arrived.

As always, I was in a good mood and Junie asked, "It's Anthony?" I said, "Yes!" "Okay, give me the phone." I waved my hand and shook my head no but this time Junie was not trying to hear me. Junie snatched the phone an said, "Hello Anthony, what up?" Anthony said, "Hey! What up with you? Have you been taking care of my woman?" I noticed that Junie's was getting red. Anthony continued, "Junie don't you ever put a hand on her or I will hurt you." Junie dropped the telephone. I picked up the phone and finished my conversation with Anthony. "Well, he seemed like he is okay," Anthony said sarcastically. "I'll speak to you tomorrow," I said and hung up the phone. I ran to the room to ask Junie what Anthony said. Junie replied angrily, "You heard it. I had him on speaker but Anthony must think that I'm some kind of punk. I guess he don't know that we live together and that I am in charge so you better tell him soon." Junie stormed out of the house and I didn't see him until the next day.

Junie's departure helped give me time to get my head right. I went downstairs to my father and asked for advice. My father looked at me and said, "You got yourself in some kind of trouble you can't get out of. First off, Anthony is a man with honor. He may be in the streets but he has a lot of honor. For him to except the things you are doing, he must have some deep love for you because he does not walk away. But for the situation that you are in, Anthony deserves for you to tell him the truth. Don't string Anthony along, tell him everything. It may hurt but be the woman that I raised you to be. Be for real. You don't have to hide. You are not married to Anthony or Junie. Baby girl, you are 28 years old. You are grown and about to make decisions for yourself as long as these men know that I will kill one of them if they hurt you." That was some good advice. I thanked and kissed my dad, and went back upstairs to my house and went to sleep on the decision that I was about to make. "March comes in like a lamb and goes out like a lion," it was the longest month that year. Junie arrived the following morning as I was going to work. We had a brief conversation and Junie told me that he needed to speak to me after I got home from work. Most women would have been mad about their man getting home the next morning but not I. I was a fly pregnant woman and besides I had been dealing with a hustler for a long time that it was something I was accustomed to. I went on to work making the best of my day then after work I stopped by Rosie's house to shoot the breeze with her. I stayed for a few hours then headed home. That day was the last work day for me before my first vacation week of the year. In the Department of Sanitation, we had eighteen days the first two years on the job. It went by seniority so March was my pick.

I was going on vacation from the March 21-28, 1992. On Saturday, March 19, I got home and Junie was not there so I decided to go back to Brooklyn and pick up my *Sue Sue*. A *Sue Sue* is when working people get together and put money in a pot and rotates the hand on the calendar so that each *Sue Sue* member would get the addition money that week. We looked at it as banking with no interest. Being that Rosie knew that I was on vacation, she convinced me to hangout with her and some of our friends from Brooklyn. I called my mother so that she didn't worry about me if she got home and I was not upstairs. Then I beeped Junie and he called me back at Rosie's house and we spoke. I told him that I would be home later. After picking up my *Sue Sue*, Rosie, Gwen, Anita, Tracey, and Linda were all going to the club and asked me to go. I told them that I would go for a little while. We went to the *Arizona Club* (not the one near the Transit building on East New York Ave) that had moved to Tapscott and Dumont (Three blocks from Rosie's house). Spending time with my girls gave me a flashback of the times we use to go out. They all had children and this was going to be my first. I was three and a half months but I was not showing because it was all in my butt. I had a big butt. As I walked into the club, I saw one of Anthony's peoples and I saw a lot of people I had not seen in a long time. I saw Bo, he was like a brother to me and Rosie but Bo was really Gwen's Brother. I saw Kenny, Pat man, and the Brownville Barber. It was just like old times in the Ville. I had about two beers and was very tore-up. I'm not a drinker so one drink gets me twisted. I decided to sit until the girls were ready to leave. I sat in a chair that was near a table that they had food on it. Before I could bat my eyes, I felt something hit my ankle. I was drunk so I didn't know what was occurring. All I remember was Tracy asking me if I alright and I said yeah. Tracy said, "They are shooting and you are in the middle." When she said that, I asked her to check my ankle. It felt like a chair hit me but I was drunk. Tracey looked down and she looked up at me a said, "No, you were not shot!" But then she picked me up and took me to her truck. I recall us driving in the wrong lane on Linden Blvd to Brookdale Hospital. I had been shot in the ankle and the Police asked me if I knew who had shot me. "I was not really conscious. I remember someone saying they would pay me as long as I don't tell but I don't remember who it was," I said to the Police Officer. I must have been looking at the shorter but I was drunk that I don't remember him.

It was hard to tell my parents and Junie what happened because they would not expect me to make such a foolish mistake. My beeper was going off at 8:30 a.m. Sunday morning. I knew Junie and my parents wanted to know where I was so Tracy offered to call my parents first. I will deal with Junie later. Tracey called my parents and they were livid. My mom said, "How do you leave and have a man that lives with you and you don't come home," all in one breathe. Tracey said, "Mom it's Tracey." "Where is Fita?" "She is in the hospital." My parents asked if something went wrong with the pregnancy and Tracey said, "No, she got shot." "Is she alright?" "Yes, she's in Brookdale hospital," Tracey replied. Rosie called Junie because Tracey didn't know Junie. Junie picked up and said, "You think that you're cute going out and not coming home. You want to do what I do?" Rosie said, "Junie this is not Fita. It's Rosie." "Where's Fita?" "In the hospital." Junie said, "What happened? Is it the baby?" "No, she has been shot," Rosie replied. Junie screamed, "NO...!" Rosie said, "She is in Brookdale Hospital and when you get yourself together, call me back so I can give you directions." Junie was from Staten Island so he wasn't familiar with Brooklyn.

At 12:00 p.m., I woke up in the hospital and I saw a lot of people around me and I said, "What is going on?" Rosie said, "Fita you was shot it the club last night." Junie was in tears along with everyone else. I asked Junie, "Where are my parents?" He said, "I told them I will take you home but I have to call them to tell them that you are alright because your mother had to stay with your father. You know he is sick." There I was in the hospital and my man was there, all of Anthony's peoples, and my friends. The hospital was very noisy and at the time I was not aware that police was watching over my room. There was also an officer gathering information about the shooting from my guest. Rosie whispered in my ear that there was an undercover cop in the room because I was the only person who was shot that survived. I closed my eyes and thanked God for my survival.

By 6:45 p.m., I was discharged me from the hospital. I said my farewells to the girls and went with Junie home. Junie drove and we talked about what had happened to me and I didn't know what to say but "Thank you for being there." That Sunday, I got home and the telephone rang. It was a collect call from Anthony. He asked, "Are you alright?" "Yes, how did you find out?" Anthony said, "You saw my people and of course they told me." "Well, call me back later. I need to get comfortable and take a shower. I gotta' unwind." Anthony said, "Tell Junie I said thanks." As I hung up the telephone, Junie asked, "Who was that?" I said, "Anthony." "What does he want?" "He just wanted to know if I was alright," I replied. Junie said, "How did he find out?" "Well, his workers were there last night and his cousin." Junie then got upset and said, "Well, were you there with his people?" "No! But Anthony has family all over." After speaking with my parents, Junie took me upstairs and made me some soup and tea. Junie then left and went to Jersey Street. At 2:30 a.m., Junie arrived home and I was sleep but he decide to wake me up. "What's wrong?" I asked. Junie said, "I am very upset with you. I feel like I'm just your man until

Anthony comes home." I said, "Junie, I'm sorry if I have you thinking that I don't love you but I do love you. It's just that I'm in love with Anthony too. I didn't think that you think someone could be in love with two people but you can. It's difficult for me to give up 5 years off my life with a man to start over, and I'm trying to do that but you need to help me. If you start getting insecure then it will make me insecure and unsure about us also." Junie understood and we cuddled and went to sleep.

The next morning I woke up in pain and Junie was there to help me. I started to realize that it was time to put things in perspective and I thought about who was around for me most. Therefore, I apologized to Junie. I told him that I would be more supportive of him being there for me and would let Anthony know that we were going to stay together. Also, I would mention that Anthony and I would have to let go of the plans we had. I told Junie to make sure he accepted the collect calls, regardless of Anthony's attitude, so that I'd be able to speak with him. Junie agreed and said, "I know that you will always be Anthony's friend." That was nice of Junie. I thanked him for understanding.

During the week of my vacation, Junie and I didn't really get into anything. Besides, I was recovering from being shot. Junie asked me if I wanted to meet his twins and I said yes. "Will it be a problem if I brought my sons over?" he asked. "No, please bring them" I replied. Junie smiled and said, "It will give you some practice for our child." "Yeah right, I don't need practice." Junie laughed and then left to pick-up his twins. I laid back down and went to sleep. At 5:00 p.m., the doorbell rang. I first got up and looked out the window and saw Junie with the twins. He couldn't open the door because his hands were full with the kids' and the baby bags that included diapers, a change of clothes, and food. As I hopped down the steps, I could see the excitement on Junie's face to be with his sons. At the time, the twins were 6 months old and they were gorgeous. They were fine little boys and happy at that. There names were Tayquan and Equan and Junie had nick named them Tay and Inkie. When I opened the door, the kids had a big smile. They seemed so lovable. I asked Junie where was their mother and he wasn't sure... "She left the boys with my mother last week and I don't know where she went. I don't care. It's not my business. I have my boys every weekend anyway and I don't mind keeping them. I am happy."

The twins stayed with us during my week vacation. However, I was not going back to work for a while as a result of my injuries. I was on bed rest until the wound on my ankle heeled, and I would have to go back to the doctor to get it approved before I went back on regular duty.

The week went by, and Junie and I had a very intense yet lovely week with the twins. The intensity came with Anthony's calls each day, asking me questions that I was not ready or willing to answer.

It was the last week of March and my father was getting sick again. Anthony called asking me if it was going to be him or Junie. I was sick with the pregnancy, Junie going crazy with my bull, and the twins were handful. It was just too much for me. Therefore, I decided to relieve my pressure. During that stressful time, Anthony called and was talking stupid so I let him have it. "Anthony you are not going to talk down about Junie no more. I love Junie and we are engaged to be married...I spend a lot of time with his twins and they are here now. I would like some peace." Anthony was silent on the other end of the telephone. After about 15 full minutes he asked, "So when did you two get engaged?" I said, "He brought me the ring for Valentine's Day." "So when were you going to tell me." "I was trying to tell you about a month ago but all you wanted to do was have phone sex." Anthony then asked, "Are you happy?" "Yes!" I replied. "I will call you later Fita." "Okay." I knew I had hurt Anthony and it was hard for him to hear what I said but I felt better. I knew that he would not call for a while. At 11:00 p.m., Junie returned home and I sat him down to talk. I said, "Well, I don't think that Anthony will be calling anymore." "Why?" Junie asked. "Well, I let him know that I love you and that we were engaged." Junie was shocked and glad that I had finally stood up for him. But what Junie didn't know was that I had fallen so much in love with him I was ready to untie the knot I had with Anthony. Junie hugged and kissed me. We then fed the twins and put them bed. Junie fed our child as we made love until the next morning. Without any sleep, we fed the twins again and went to sleep as a family.

That afternoon, my mother went upstairs and asked that Junie drive her and my father to the hospital while I stayed home with the twins. April was a heavy month on my pregnancy. I was four months and was running to the hospital with my mother for my father constantly. He had gotten sicker. I was also in and out of court with Junie he decided to take the twins mother to court to gain custody of them. The trial was a difficult road to go down but we won the case and the twins were ours. It was time to go shopping. I turned the guest room into the twins' bedroom. By May, I was happy and comfortable with my new profound life. I hadn't heard from Anthony and things were going well. I was engaged, happy, in love, and had my twins and was expecting my own child. My man was good and he loved me. But May was the month that my family found out my father was not going to make it. I was a daddy's girl. The news hit me hard but I tried to be strong for my mother. From there on out, each weekend the entire family would visit my dad - my brother Junior, his wife Vicky and their children Victoria, James, and Stephanie, my aunts Sarah and Paquita, Uncle Mimo, my cousins Leon and Clarissa and Sean (Clarissa's husband), as well as Junie and the twins. We wanted to make my father happy and maybe God would cure him (at least that's what I wanted). On May 9, 1992, we left the hospital and I remember having a funny feeling in my stomach. I looked at my mother and said, "Don't be surprised if you get a call from the hospital on mother's day, which was the next day.

On May 10th, my mother received a call from the hospital to pick-up my dad's items. Daddy had gone home with the Lord. When my mother called upstairs to my house at 8:00 a.m., I was lying in the bed and already knew what she was calling me for. Instead of picking up the telephone, I got out of bed and ran downstairs. Junie was up and ready to go with me to take my mother to the hospital and left the twins with my brother and his wife. My mother got to the hospital and dealt with the arrangements in reference to the burial. From the hospital, we drove to Brooklyn to announce my father's death to my aunts and uncles houses to (my father was born into a family of ten). Afterward, we went back to the Island to prepare for what was to come.

On Monday morning, my mom and I went to the funeral home to pay for the burial fees and then went shopping for my father's attire. Death on Mother's Day wasn't the best feeling but got us through it. By Tuesday, the viewing along with the burial went well. There were speakers and vocalist, and overall everyone was pleased.

A week later, I was cleaning my house and I heard the telephone ring over my loud music. I was home alone with the twins while Junie was on The Ave. Nonetheless, I stopped what I was doing to answer the phone and it was Anthony. "My condolences, I heard daddy passed away." "Yeah, he did," I replied. Anthony asked, "Are you ok?" "Yes, but I'm still going through the shock of my father really being dead." "I know you was his baby girl...How you and Junie doing?" I said, "Good." Anthony said, "I had a dreamt that you were pregnant." I replied, "Boy you crazy!" "Are you pregnant?" "No!" Anthony said, "I will talk to you later." I don't know why I didn't tell him the truth but I couldn't hurt him anymore. Afterward, I imagined my father telling me don't lead him on if you not going to wait tell him. I kept hearing his voice that over and over.

Around 6:00 p.m., the telephone rang and it was a correctional facility operator. It was Anthony again. He asked, "What are you Doing?" "Watching TV." I replied. "Where's Junie?" "Out." Anthony said, "Well, now that you are a mother with twins, Junie keeps you in the house. He not showing you off anymore." I said, "Anthony what's wrong with you?" Anthony said, "Well, I know you better than you think I do. I asked you a question and you laughed when answering, and the answer didn't sit well in my stomach.

Anthony mentioned his dream again and said that my father was also in it so he asked the question again. I stopped watching TV and said "Anthony I am 5 months pregnant." Anthony screamed, "WHAT THE HELL!" and hung up. An hour and half later, Junie got home and we talked about our relationship. To me, he had a funny look on his face. The I'm sleeping around with someone else look (as if there was someone else in his life). I asked, "Junie, what's up?" He said, "What are you talking about?" "You usually come home to stay but tonight you are going back out on The Ave." "I have to watch my money" I said, "You never watch your money, it's always there" Junie didn't know what to say. He gathered his thoughts and replied, "You must have talked to Anthony." "No, you are looking very guilty." Junie stormed out.

The next day, I got up and took a shower, got dressed and went to Brooklyn. I decided to leave Junie with the twins. At 6:30 p.m., I was driving back to Shaolin from BK and decided to go through Bay St. and there were about four girls flagging my car down. I had no clue who the hell they were so I rolled up on them slowly and they all looked surprised to see a female in the car. That's when I realized Junie was playing me. The only thing I could think of was that they thought I was him. From that day on, I never trusted Junie again. I started to accept Anthony's calls again and we enjoyed long conversations. I refrained from telling Anthony why I was accepting his call again. Junie couldn't understand the change my attitude. I was still the twins' mother and took care of them as they grew bigger. The boys and I did everything together. I was going on 6 months and Anthony and I were really getting close. Finally, I told Anthony about the incident with the girls that had happened a month prior. Anthony said, "Well, you really never got to know Junie. You and him just jumped the gun. So what are you going to do - he's not going home, he is in the street all the time, the both of you argue so much in front of the boys. It's not a go look." I said, "I don't know." Anthony asked, "Why would you have gotten pregnant from someone you really don't know?" "It was on the first night and I was not getting an abortion. I'm too old for that. I need to go on. Anthony you had lied to me and you was still messing with Becky. I love you Anthony but I can't let you play me anymore." "I love you too. Why do you think I never let you get away from me? I never loved a woman the way I love you," he replied. Anthony and I grew closer as Junie and I grew apart. It got so bad that Junie decided to move back to his mother's house with the twins.

For the next two weeks, I spoke to Anthony and we were inseparable again. It had been two months without sleeping with Junie, and one month since the twins lived with us. Anthony asked, "Fita, why don't you wait for me to get home and have my baby." I said, "Anthony, I am 6 months. I can't go get an abortion now" "If you love me, you will wait," he replied. I started to cry and I said, "What do you want me to do?" Anthony said, "Get rid of it and I will give you a baby. I don't think I could be with you if you have someone else's baby. Let's just do what we always wanted to do, have our children together." At that time, the phone was going to cut off and I said bye. That night, I was in tears and could not believe that he had asked me to get an abortion. The sad thing is, for a second, I considered it for the love of Anthony. I cried all night but I wanted my man; the man that I had loved for 6 years of my life and I wanted him forever.

I called my best friend Rosie because I needed to speak with her. I woke her up crying and told her what Anthony had asked of me. Roise was silent. She then said, "I will love you forever, whatever your decision is but I can't help you make that decision. It's too much for me to swallow." It took me about one week before I could make a decision. During that time, I denied Anthony's collect calls. I thought about not wanting to raise a baby by myself. Junie was no longer in the picture. I couldn't speak to my mother about the situation because she would have killed me for considering the option. A week before my birthday, I decided to go ahead with the procedure. I called Rosie to inform her of my decision. The plan was that I would go to Gwen's house. She lived by herself. Gwen would be taking me to the hospital, and I would tell my mother that I was at Rosie's.

On May 30, 1992, I woke up and told my mother I was going to spend the night with Rosie because we were going out. My mother wasn't stupid. I believe she knew what I was going do and was very much against it. I then got in my car and I drove to Gwen's. She lived on Halsey Street between Evergreen and Wilson in Brooklyn. I got to Gwen's house and she asked if I was ready and I said yes.

The next day, I walked into the abortion clinic on Queens Blvd and I got on that operating table. I let them insert a sixteen-six up inside my vagina, which would cause me to go into labor because I was so far along in my pregnancy. I had to stay at Gwen's for two days until the baby was ready to come out. I suffered two days of what's considered labor pains and on June 3rd it was over. I had killed my child for the love of a man. It was different for me. Some people get high or drink their depression away but I would party so I didn't have to think about what happens to me. Therefore, when I got to my house, I cried until my birthday on the 5th. I called up all my girls from Brooklyn and asked them to go out to the club with me. My girls loved me. They were very depressed about my situation but agreed to hang-out on the Island. We went to club *Consequence*. The place was crowded but I was okay with that because I needed to be around people because so that I wouldn't dwell on what I had done.

When we got into club *Consequence* and Rosie said she had seen Junie and he asked for me. I ignored her statement and went to the bar to get a drink. That's when I saw Junie who was in front of me. He said,"What are you doing?" "I'm having a drink." "But you're pregnant." "Junie I lost the baby last week," I replied. Junie looked at me and asked, "When were you going to call me to tell me?" I said, "I didn't think it was any of your concern being that you were out doing your thing." Junie left the club that night upset. I paid him no mind and enjoyed my birthday. The girls and I drank and danced. However, I began feeling pains so Rosie and Gwen made sure I got home safely.

It took me about a month to get over what I had done. I never forgave myself but I had to get back to work and back to my life. Ms. Independent went back to work full duty and continued to make money to stack up. After the third week in June, I began accepting calls from Anthony again. "Hi!" "Why have you not accepted my calls," he asked. I said, "I needed to get myself together. That was some heavy suggestions you put on me." "So I guess you're still pregnant. When do you go in?" he asked. I said, "When you put me in there." Anthony's voice totally changed. He said, "You got the abortion?" I said, "Yes, I love my man and I wanted his baby." Anthony said, "Well, I was coming home July but I had a fight last month so I will be home in September." "You are still fighting?" "It was when you told me about your pregnancy. I was mentally messed up. I had to take my anger out on someone and I got some more time. But it's only two extra months." I said, "Okay Anthony but don't get in no more trouble." He coughed and said, "You don't get in anymore trouble."

For the next month, I worked hard and tried to get myself together. It was hard trying not to think about my child but it was too late now. I had made the decision and I would have to live with it for the rest of my life. Nevertheless, I had to try and put it behind me as well as Junie. By July, I had gotten back into the swing of things. I was focused and prepared for my man to return home. I wanted to be ready for him.

During the month of July, I reminisced about the conversation I

had with Anthony when he first told me he was going to be home
on July 5th but because of the fight he wasn't going to be released.
Nevertheless, I hoped for a call from him saying he was out and that he
was on his way to see me but of course that didn't happen. Each day, I
found myself having weird feelings as if he was out but he wasn't.
Towards the end of August, I received a call from Anthony and he had
said that he would be home soon but he didn't give me a date. It was ok
that he wasn't home because I was working and keeping myself busy.

August weather was in full effect. It was hot and I was working
in the heat. This particular August was very hot and I would complete
my route and go straight home. Sanitation was canceling some of the
chart (days off) and they needed manpower for the holidays. I was so
focus that I had not realized Labor Day weekend had arrived and
September was here.

My mom called me at work and asked if I was going straight
home after work and I said yes. She asked, "What did you wear to
work?" I said, "A sweat suit." "When you get home please take a
shower and put something nice on because I need you to take me
somewhere." I said okay but I wanted to skip out because I was tired
and it was hot. When I got home, my brother asked to use my car and I
said no. I then went upstairs and jumped in the shower to dress myself in
my blue and white bermuda shorts set with and sandals. I looked so
cute. Afterward, I went to my mother's house and asked if she was
ready. My mother said "Well yes but your brother took your car keys." I
screamed, "I TOLD HIM NOT TO TAKE MY CAR KEYS." "Well,
go on upstairs until he comes back and I will get the keys from. Because
if you stay down here you will argue with him and I don't want to be
bothered."

As I passed the front door to go upstairs to my apartment, I
looked out through the doors window and saw my brother parking my
car and Anthony was with him. I opened the door to look and make sure
I saw correctly and that my eyes were not deceiving me. I shouted,
"ANTHONY!" and we both ran to each other. We looked like we were
in a commercial where two lovers fun toward each other in slow motion.
That's what if felt like. I was surprised see Anthony. My brother went to
pick Anthony up at the Staten Island Ferry. At the time, that was the
best surprise of my life. I had no idea that Anthony and my family were
keeping secrets from me. When my mother saw Anthony and the look
on my face, she said "I think you guys have a lot to discuss." Anthony
said, "Not yet mom. I want to know if you are alright and I 'm sorry that
I was not around for daddy's death. I'm concerned about you. Are you
alright mommy?" Mommy said, "Anthony, thank you. You and Fita

have a lot to talk about. You and her need to go upstairs. The family is glad that you are home." Anthony kissed my mother and shook my brother's hand, "Thank you Junior!" And my brother replied, "No problem, just keep my sister happy." Anthony and I went upstairs and we talked. It was not a sex or jump in bed kind of thing, we needed to really talk.

Anthony took is clothes off and got comfortable. I cooked as we talked and rekindled our love for one another. At 6:00 p.m., I asked Anthony what he wanted to do. He said, "Well, let's go to Brooklyn. I want to see my father." "Now to BK?" "Yes!" I never asked Anthony where the clothes he had for the past three years were. I guess I was excited to see him so it didn't matter. Anthony was home and I was happy. Nevertheless, we drove to Brooklyn to see his father. As we entered Brooklyn, Anthony began to call his peoples that he had not seen since he was locked up; at least that's what I thought. I asked, "Why you are calling them if you haven't seen them in a long time. They didn't go see you." Anthony said, "We kept in touch because business is business." We made a couple of stops and then went to Brownsville around St John and Ralph and Buffalo to his father. It was getting late and I asked Anthony if he was ready to go home. He said, "You go mommy. I will be home tomorrow. I want to stay with my father." I was highly upset he had just got home, and we hadn't had one night together. I was frustrated and angry. I could not understand what had occurred. I went on home upset and I didn't even beep him.

The next morning, a Parole Officer was ringing my doorbell. I did not expect them that early and not on the second day. He asked me where was Anthony and I said, "I took him to his father's house this morning." He then asked me if I had any guns in the house. I looked at him and said no. He then said, "I would like to check your entire house." And I told him it was okay to do so. But I asked him why? The Parole Officer said that Anthony was on parole for gun charges so if there were any guns in the house, he would go back to prison. There cannot be any guns on his premises.

I beeped Anthony to tell him that there was a parole officer at the house. Anthony asked, "What did you say?" "I said I took you to Brooklyn to your father's house this morning." Anthony replied, "That's my girl. You have all the answers." While I was talking to Anthony, the Parole Officer was still checking the house. He was all in the closets but then it dawned on me that Junie had his shot gun up in the room closet. I started to pray in my head, "Oh God, please I don't need any problems for Anthony. Oh God, once again God answer my prayers." God came through because they didn't find the shot gun. Every room was clear.

The officer said, "Tell Anthony that next time to be home." "Will do," I replied. They left the house and I was glad. I just wanted to find the shotgun and get it out of my house. As I looked in all the closets upstairs, it was no where to be found. However, I went to the basement and sure enough it was their. I beeped Junie and I told him to meet me on Westervelt so I could give him his gun. I told him to have somewhere to put it because it couldn't stay in my house. When I got to Westervelt to meet Junie, I handed him the bag and then he said, "What up?" I said, "Anthony's home." Junie was upset. "Well, when he come home today tell him I want to meet him." I said, "No you don't." Junie said, "Yes I do." "Whatever Junie," I said and then I left. When I got home, my phone rang and it was Anthony. "Where were you? I called a little while go." I said, "Well, I was at mommy's house." "Okay, I will be ready to go home about 5:00 p.m. so pick me up at my father's," he replied.

It was 4:00 p.m. and I had cleaned my house and cooked. It was time for me to shower and get ready to pick-up Anthony. I arrived to Brooklyn by 5:00 p.m. and Anthony waiting. He got in the car and we went straight home. Anthony got in the shower and then he ate. Later, he wanted to play (have sex). I was down because it was time that I released what I had been holding on for. We played with each other as we kissed and then it happened. Anthony started mumbled my name and I was called his too. After we made love we showered together, and then watched a movie and just chilled.

At about 10:00 p.m., the doorbell rung and I looked at Anthony. He said, "That is not for me. No one knows where I live." I said, "It's not for me either." I slowly crept my way downstairs to get the door and it was Junie. I was shocked. "What do you want Junie?" He said, "I want to meet the man." I said, "Daddy, it's for you." Anthony asked, "Who is it?" "Junie." "Tell him I will be down. Let me put some clothes on." Anthony said that loud enough for Junie to hear.

When Anthony got downstairs, he shook Junie's hand and they went upstairs into my living room to talk like men. I went in the bedroom and waited an hour until they were done speaking. Junie left and Anthony met me in the room. I never questioned what was said because I played my part as woman. But I was torn between two lovers because I was still in love with Junie too. They had both played a large role in my life. Anthony was my man for life. He promised my father that he'd take care of me. Junie was my man that was there for me when I needed a man the most. Through rough times and we share a baby for 6 months.

Anthony stayed at home for about three weeks before he went

running the streets with his business again. During the three weeks Anthony and I were inseparable, we did everything together just like I always wanted. We went out on the town, movies and shopping, and had candle light dinners. We became romantic once again. I had done no wrong. Anthony had forgiven me for my mistake and that was all I needed to know. We went to Far Rockaway pick up money and engage in plenty of love making but back to Anthony on the grind for his money. That's when I started staying home. I had plenty of lonely nights and saw him only in the morning when he would take me and pick me up from work. Although I was lonely, I was glad that he was home. I knew that he was building his stash for the both of us. But I must admit those lonely nights had me thinking what else he was doing out in the street, which lead me to find out he was cheating on me again. One day, I beeped Anthony at 4:30 a.m. to remind him that I had to work. I had not heard from him all night so I waited for my call back. Anthony called back and said, "I'm on my way." As I was getting dressed, the phone rang. I said, "Hello!" but the person hung up. It rang again and I said, "Hello!" and behold there was an angry woman on the other end. She sucked her teeth and said, "I hate you!" I was stunned.

Anthony arrived about 40 minutes later and I got in the car and refrained from mentioning the call until we got to BK. I said, What ever or who ever you were with called the house and cursed me out." Anthony acted shocked and said, "So you think I'm messing around?" "Well, I don't do women." "What you are saying? Is that where you think that I was; at a woman's house and she got mad that I got up out of her bed to pick my woman up." "Yes," I said and unexpectedly, Anthony slapped me so hard, I saw stars. I was in disbelief. We were together for 7 years and he never hit me. I was so furious that I punched him in his penis as he was driving and we almost got into an accident. I went into work and I never called him to pick me up.

I had completed my route at about 10:00 a.m. I dumped the truck and I went back to the garage to shower and decided to go to Rosie's house. I asked my supervisor to put in a four hour comp-time to complete the pay wage for the day. And at 2:00 p.m., my supervisor and some of my co-workers beeped me to tell me that my man was outside waiting on me. I told them to tell Anthony that I was not there. I knew that I had to get home and since I never had taken the Staten Island Ferry since moving to the Island, I decided that day would be my day to try it.

Rosie asked, "What is this surprise visit? Since your Anthony's been home, no one has seen or heard from you...So what is up pimp?! In an angry tone, I went on to tell her that I had been played. "He is messing around, and you know what you do in the dark comes out in the light!" Rosie said, "Slow down and park." I told her what had happened. I even told her about the slap. Rosie said, "Well, he messing around. I'm not feeling that nor the slap... You don't think that the slap came from the stuff that had happened while he was away?" I said, "He's not my father and I was faithful for 6 1/2 years and one time that I messed up. He has cheated for years.The doorbell rang and it was Anthony. Muller, Rosie's father said, "Anthony, she's not here." Muller was cool like my father (God bless the dead). I heard Anthony and Muller arguing and Anthony said, "I know she is here so tell her to come out." I walked out and said, "What is this? You're arguing with Muller?" Anthony said, "Muller started screaming 'go she don't need you'." I said, "Anthony, you know how Muller is." "I'm sorry! I didn't mean to slap you." I said, "Okay," and I got in the car and left. I didn't want to cause problems on Strauss St.

As we drove to Shaolin, I didn't say a word. I let Anthony do all the talking while I was planning my next step (a technique I learned from him). I got in the house and I went to my mother's apartment to speak with her. Afterward, I went upstairs to my bedroom, got undress, and watched TV. Anthony asked, "What are you going to do?" I said, "Nothing!" "Would you like to go out for dinner?" "No!" "Would you like to ride with me to pick up our money?" "No!" Anthony asked, "Do you need some time alone?" I said, "Yes!" "About how long?" I replied, "About a week or two." Anthony and I were Gemini's so he knew, just like I knew, when we needed space. Anthony said, "Well, I will leave your car and I will take my car (1990 735 BMW Black on Black). "Okay!" Anthony kissed me on the cheek and left.

For the next two weeks, Anthony and I spoke, and we went out but I never forgot the smack on the face. I beeped Anthony one afternoon for my mother. She wanted him to pick her up a (VCR) from Sears. They were having a sale and instead of Anthony calling me back, it was a girl's voice, "Yes, who is calling my husband?" I said, "Who is this?" The female said, "Becky!" "Becky, put Anthony on the phone." "He asked me to answer all his calls." I said, "I bet that if he knew you answered my call he would kill you so I suggest that you just give him the phone." Anthony got on the phone and said, "It ain't what you think?" I said, "Forget it!" and hung up. Anthony called back I said, "You have a lot of nerves having that whore answer your calls." After hanging up, the phone rung again and it was Becky calling from a phone booth and she had the nerve to be arguing with my mother. I snatched the phone from my mother's hand and promised Becky that I would whip her ass when I saw her. After that day, I told Anthony that he couldn't stay with me anymore. I told him to pick his clothes up, he would find them on my front steps.

Anthony never picked his clothes that day but about a week later he went to my house and I was around the corner on Jersey St. talking to Junie. We were just chatting, small talk, when I saw Anthony's car ride by. I had no respect for him so I didn't care. He let that witch talk the way she wanted to my mother and me. I told Junie that I would check him later and Junie agreed. I went to my house and found Anthony's car was gone and so were his clothes. I felt more at ease. I had called a locksmith and changed the locks just in case he tried to return. I was no fool.

I had made it my business to stay away from Anthony. I kept my butt in Shaolin and didn't go to Brooklyn much, only to see my girls once in a while. In October of 1992, I had finally got my transfer and was working on Staten Island. I was the first woman and minority on the Island. I even made news in the Staten Island Advance newspaper. It was a big thing on the Island and I was proud. At that time, I started seeing Junie again. We decided to take things slow that time around. We both realized that we had moved too fast in the past.

We had been together for six weeks and things had been going well. He would visit me at my place often and we would go out all the time. One day, we were on our way to the movies and I felt sick. I began to throw up. Needless to say, we never made it to the movies but instead Junie took me to the doctor's office. The flu had been going around that year so we wanted to make sure I got treated early if that was my diagnosis. I'm sure just getting over my menstrual cycle had something to do with me not feeling well too. After getting checked out, Junie and I waited for my results and the doctor said, "Ms. McEachin you're pregnant." Junie looked at me happy as hell but I wasn't happy. The doctor continued to say, "You need to be on bed-rest. We have to run some more test because you are a high risk. There was an operation that you had that caused you some problems. You'll have to stay in bed." I looked at Junie and Junie asked the doctor if I was six weeks and the doctor said, "No." "Four weeks?" The doctor said, "She's ten weeks. Congrats!" Junie looked at me and I was shocked, nauseous, upset, and embarrassed that Junie took me to the hospital to find out I was pregnant but it wasn't his. Why God? Junie asked, "What do you want me to do?" I said, "Whatever you'd like." (You could leave if you'd like) "I love you so I will raise the baby with you. No one has to know," he replied.

I had to stay in the hospital for testing so Junie left, returning the next day. All night thought about the situation that I was in and decided to call the baby's father. I beeped Anthony and he called back, "Who is this?" I said, "Anthony?" "Yeah, what up Fita?" "I'm in the hospital." He asked, "What's wrong?" "I'm pregnant," I replied. "And...Junie is acting stupid or something?" "How you know that I'm with Junie?" Anthony said, "I know your every move." I said, "Okay, forget that...the baby is yours." "WHAT?!" The what was a good what. He sounded excited. "How many months?" "Two and a half." Anthony said, "So what are you going to do?" "Junie said that he'll raise the baby with me," I replied. Anthony then hung up. I guess I insulted him.

I stayed in the hospital for two days and when I returned to work I was on light duty. Anthony called me a week later at my job and told me that he wanted to see me in Brooklyn when I got off of work and I agreed. I met Anthony on Willoughby and Bridge St. in front of Brooklyn North Borough Office - The Dept. of Sanitation. Anthony asked, "Are you hungry?" "No but I will get something," I replied. Nevertheless, I had a taste for shrimp and french fries.

After he bought our food, we sat in his car and ate. "Do you think it's fare that Junie raise my baby?" he asked. I said, "No." "So why would you even mention that?" "Well I know that we can't be together and I didn't want any problems." Anthony asked, "What problems?" "I don't need no drama with Becky in an out of my life," I replied. Anthony said, "So you think that I would let Junie raise my baby." I said, "Where are you going with the question?" "It's not hard for me to dump Becky. But the question is can you leave Junie?...I have never worried about you with men. In the past, you were faithful but I have noticed that Junie is very competitive to me. I also noticed that you are in love with the both of us so it would really be hard for you. I am leaving it in your hands. I am willing to forgive you of all that was done because I know that I deserved it with my track record but it's on you. I do want my family back so I will give you some time to think about it." I looked at Anthony and said, "Thank you!" I got out of his car a got into mine and went home.

It was November and I had not made a decision so Anthony called me and said that it was time that he makes the decision and he was coming home. I didn't let Junie know that Anthony was coming over (I had forgotten). Therefore, when Junie came to see me, Anthony answered the door and they got into a big argument outside of my house. I didn't know what to do. My mom didn't get into because she told me this day would come. Two workers from the 24 hour gas station, George and Omar, stopped the fight before the cops arrived. Afterward, Anthony calmed and went upstairs to get in bed. Anthony said, "Junie will not be coming around anymore." I said, "Anthony are you going to take me to the doctor's? Are you going to be a family man? Are you going to take care of home before the streets?" but no response. I asked these questions because I knew Junie would do all of the above. As time went on and I started to get sicker but Anthony began taking me to the doctor's and started becoming the man of my choice again.

By December, I was about five months pregnant and I had to go for a sonogram. I was not feeling good and I did not feel the baby move as often. I felt like it hadn't done so for about a week, I got nervous. Anthony had to go to Brooklyn but went with me to the doctor's first. The nurses ran special test on me and the result came back, "Ms. McEachin, I'm sorry but the baby is dead." Anthony looked at me in tears, and I cried leaving the doctor's office. I looked up at the sky and said, "I'm sorry God for what I have done." I looked at Anthony and he said, "We will have a baby. We'll try again mami." Anthony didn't go to Brooklyn but stayed home with me instead.

Anthony tried with all of his might to cheer me up. What he did realize was that it was a punishment for what we had done to ourselves and each other. God had given me a gift, which was a baby before and I killed it for Anthony. God was a jealous God and he said don't put no man before him and I had done everything in my life for the strength of Anthony, which was another man and not God. For me to carry a baby for 5 months and the baby be dead, what more could I have dealt with in this life? This kept me down for weeks. I went into depression. If it wasn't for Victoria, Stephen and Chino (nieces & nephew), Junior (Brother) and Vickie (Sister-In-Law), I would not know what it was to have children in a household. The fun in raising them I thanked God for.

Anthony went to Far Rockway after about two weeks because I needed to pull it together but had to be alone. As I went back to work on regular duty, it was winter time. The weather was cold and snowy; it was "blood money season." Work gave me time to get things right and focused. I was plowing snow for 12 hours a day; there was no time to think dwell on things. There was so much snow I didn't have much time off and didn't see Anthony often. We talked more than once a day. I kinda' felt as if he had someone in his life, but I was okay with just being friends. It had been such a long year and I was thrown so many curve balls. I was glad that a new year was near.

Chapter XI

After the Storm

Anthony said, "What time will you be home? Can we go out or get together?" I said, "Yes. I won't have to go to work tonight so maybe we can get into something special." When I got home around four o'clock, I got right in the shower to prepare myself for an evening with my man. I had been denying him of his pleasures because I was working so much. Instead, I was getting a lot of attention from my colleagues. The men at work always made the women on the job feel special; at least they made me feel wanted and needed. I felt loved and joy. We were a family, even though it was a rough road getting the men at the job to believe that women can be just as strong as they are. Believe you me, it was definitely a hard job but the women at the garage were willing to prove there strength. It was the 90's, and it was a new day for every city job. There had been a big push for diversity and women. We were jumping into positions that white men had held down for years. There's nothing women can't do. Women were in charge. Sanitation opened up many doors for women within other city departments. Power to women!

At six o'clock, Anthony picked me up and we went to dinner and a movie. We hadn't gone out in about three months. After our date, we went to his house to talk and I asked him about Becky. Anthony said, "You would not understand?" I heard this line before. Anthony went on to tell me that, "Becky does anything that I ask." I said, "Then you must want a puppet for a girl." "No, that's why I could never be faithful to a woman that is not competitive to me. Becky is just someone that I spend time with being that it's convenient." I asked, "Baby, when are you going to grow up? I don't want the fast life anymore. I'm getting to old to be as worried as I've been. We go through these ups and downs with our relationship and I need you to let the street life go…Baby, I love you but I'm scared that one day I will have to bury you. I don't want to be alone." Anthony looked in my eyes and said, "Baby, I love you too but I have been doing this all my life." "Why you don't go back to the studio. Anthony you have a skills. You have an ear for music." "Fita, when we were young it was alright for you. Now, it's hard for you to accept," he replied. I said, "Yes, you are an M.C. and you are wasting your talent. Why?" There was a pause and I began to cry, and continued to say, "They (the government) are not playing. They are giving you a hard time for that stuff. I'm scared so it's either me or the life." Anthony looked at me with tears in his eyes and said, "Let's just enjoy this night and we will talk about it tomorrow."

Anthony and I made love the whole night until day and we had breakfast and went back to sleep. Never once did we speak on topic again. I noticed that we had gone our separate ways following this day. Well, I went on with my life, working and getting into my career within the department. I started to really get involved with the people I was working with. The rest of the women and I on the staff began an organization. We became very active within sanitation. I had received a call on the job. It was kind of strange but I answered the telephone.

"Hello! McEachin speaking "

The voice said, "Oh! Don't you sound so professional."

I said, "Who is this?"

The man said, "Fita, so you don't know my voice?"

I said, "Hey! What up baby?" It was Anthony.

He said, "I need to talk to you. When do you get home?"

"Well, I have to work a twelve hour shift, it's mandatory. This is winter hours and it's snowing. You know how that goes."

Anthony said, "Okay. I will see you tomorrow."

I went back to work but couldn't help to think about what he wanted to talk to me about. I had not seen him in a few months. After work, I went home. I was very tired. I had a long week ahead of me but I had a long weekend to look forward too. I wouldn't have to return to work until Tuesday. When I got home, I took a shower and went to bed.

The next morning, I woke up and called Anthony to let him know that I was ready to go out. Anthony said he had some business to take care of but afterward he would be by to pick me up. At about 9:30 p.m. on Saturday evening, Anthony picked me up and we went to his house to pick up some money and then we went to dinner.

At the dinner table, Anthony said, "Okay baby, you won my heart and I just have this one request and I will be done, and will go back into the studio. But I need you to first promise that you are with me on my decision." I said, "What is your request?" "I will have to go out of town one more time and I will quit," and I agreed that it was okay. I knew that Anthony was a good man. He had a good heart. First and fore most, I loved him and he was in love with me. We were soul mates.

I knew that no other man loved me more then he did, he just had a funny way of showing it. After our agreement, I was happy that he was going to quit so we celebrated. We went to a movie and he bought me a bottle of Moet. We then went to his house and made love. On Sunday afternoon, we spoke about the agreement again. Anthony said, "Baby, I will have to leave on Monday and I will be out of town for about one month." "Why that long?" I asked. He said, "This is it remember so I have to shut this down right, with no trace." I was going to go home that day but when Anthony told me he was leaving Monday, I stayed at his place until he left.

The next morning, I took Anthony to the greyhound bus terminal. I kissed him good-bye and asked him to call me once he arrived to his destination. Anthony was on his way to Delaware then to Philly. When I got home, I immediately prayed to God that nothing should happen to him and that God bring him back home to me to start a clean life. Amen!

For the first two weeks of Anthony's trip, things seemed fine. He would call me every night and we would talk about things that were going to happened once he returned home. But on the third week, things got funny. Anthony called me and he sounded weird. He got on the phone but it was like he really couldn't talk. He was speaking in riddles. I could hardly understand him. I had to read between the lines.

I asked, "Baby, do you need to call me on another telephone?"

Anthony said, "I'll call back in about two hours. Thank you Bonnie!"

"Okay Clyde."

"I will be home tomorrow."

"What's going on Anthony?"

"I really can't tell you but I will need you to pick me up at Jay Street in Brooklyn," he said.

"Why you don't want me to pick you up at greyhound?"

Anthony said, "Not good."

"Okay!"

Chapter XII

Last Trip

I went to work the next morning. My shift was from 6 a.m. – 2 p.m. and after work I went to the Jay Street, Boro Hall, to the A train and waited there for about 40 minutes for Anthony. But he didn't show up, remembered that he said that he was going to take an early bus.

More than an hour had passed and there was still no Anthony. I started beeping him because I was very worried but didn't hear anything back. He didn't beep me back. My imagination started to run wild. I called his house and Ms. Michelle answered.

"Mom is Anthony home?"

She said, "No."

"Did you hear from him?"

"Yes, about two days ago."

I asked, "He didn't tell you he was coming home today?"

Ms. Michelle said, "No baby."

My worries turned into anger. I was angry that he wasn't beeping me back and I was even angrier at the fact that he did not tell his mother that he was returning home on that day. If he got picked up, there was no way of knowing it until he called me. After waiting for over two hours, I went home and sat by the phone. I watch the minutes go by. Hours passed and no call from Anthony. It was time for me to go to bed.

When I got in my bed, the telephone rang. It was Rosie. "Girl, I have not seen you in a few months. Even since you transferred to Staten Island, you don't come to Brooklyn much. That job got your butt wrapped up," she said. "Girl, I have to master this job before I could fit my life around it. I have no seniority on the Island but I do like it a lot because I'm close to home. The men are crazy too. You would like them, especially since they like to party."

Rosie said, "I hear that. So what up with you and Anthony?"

"We are friends."

"What happened?" she asked.

I said, "He could not give that life he lives up."

"Okay, so you had him choose you or the life?"

"Yes!" Rosie he realized that I came first so we are trying to work it out.

Rosie said, "Cool."

"Girl, I got to go to bed. I have to work in the morning."

"I will speak to you tomorrow," she replied.

It was 5:00 a.m., and was time for me to get prepared to go to work when my beeper started going off. I grabbed it and put it on vibrate as I checked the number. It was Anthony's house. I called back and Anthony said, "I'm sorry that I had you worried but when you get home from work, I will explain." I went onto work and completed my route early. I decided that I would return back to the garage and ask to leave sooner. I spoke to my supervisor and he said it was fine. I had tons of time in the books anyway. I got dressed and went to Far Rock.

When I arrived at the building, Anthony buzzed me in immediately. As I walked up the stairs, I noticed that Anthony had already opened the door. Before I could say anything, Anthony picked me up and took me to his room where he took my clothes off and took me to heaven. After lovemaking, I looked at Anthony and smiled.

I asked, "Why you ain't call me?"

Anthony said, "I was getting on the greyhound bus to come back and I noticed two white detectives following me. I decided not to get on just to see if they were really following me."

"And…?"

"And they were so I had to stay another day until I shook them. I didn't want them to follow me on greyhound and call for assistance to search me on the bus with no room to get away."

I said, "How do you know that they have been following you?"

Anthony said, "I have seen them before."

"Anthony this is it right?"

Anthony said, "That's it."

I got in the shower and Anthony followed. He began kissing my breast and sucked on my nipples until they were hard. He made his way down my mid-section, kissing my body all the way to my vagina. Then he stuck me with his big bob. I was in heaven again. When we got out of the shower, we went to eat some franks and sausages on the boardwalk.

Anthony lived in Far Rockaway and down the block was Rockaway Playland. At 8:30 p.m. I had to go home to get ready for the next day. We left Playland and I headed home.

The next morning, I was felt good. I got some good loving from my man and we were finally on the same page again. No more hustling for Anthony. At work, my beeper went off and it was Anthony.

"You did it again," he said when I called him back.

"What are you talking about?" I asked.

"You put it on me again?"

I just laughed and said "Is that why you called me?"

He said, "No."

"Why did you beep me?"

"I just wanted to say good morning and that I love you."

I said, "Same here."

"What are your plans for the day?"

"I don't have any."

He said, "Let's go out."

"Okay!"

I was winter so I did not know where we would be going. Since, money was not a problem because that last trip that Anthony had taken he had made enough money to carry him for at least six months. Besides I was working.

Chapter XIII

A New Beginning

It was January 1993 and our relationship was perfect. Anthony and I finally put our past behind us; the bad and the good. The cheating was over. Anthony was not hustling anymore and started to book time in the studio to record his album. He was always in the studio but I didn't mind it. He was finally doing something positive and staying out of trouble. I felt like things were going to be alright. Anthony even started talking about marriage. We actually had a conversation about it several times. It was a very sensitive topic for me because before I met Anthony, I was engaged to be married but I canceled the wedding because I found out the guy cheated.

I was very nervous about marriage. I had loved Anthony too much and was afraid that marriage would change our relationship. Appose to me being engaged to Junie, I had to learned to love him but Anthony was the man of my dreams so things were different.

One month went by, and Anthony was in the studio finalizing the A side of his cassette tape for his album. I was working hard and keeping things in check. We still had to visit his parole officer once a week, which always went well.

I would hear Anthony repeat his lyrics before going into the studio. I had them down packed. I could not rhyme so I left that part to him. Nevertheless, I was happy to see him happy. He seemed very excited and focused.

By March, the A side was complete and he was working on the B side. This side was going to be more difficult. He wanted to make sure his lyrics and tracks were extra tight. Therefore, Anthony decided to take a break for a few weeks to enjoy some time with me.

Anthony helped me fix the house in Staten Island and things were good and peaceful. One Saturday night, Anthony got a call from Brooklyn. I wasn't sure who it was. All I remember was that he got dressed and told me that he would be back. I was okay with that because I knew that he was not in the business anymore so I didn't really question his whereabouts.

I later find out that Anthony had gone to Far Rockaway to an old friend's house. The friend told him that police were around Bay Towers, where Anthony use to live, questioning people about Anthony and a shooting that occurred in the 80's. Police wanted to speak to Anthony about it.

Anthony returned home and didn't say too much after explaining what happed. We ate and made love. Although he said things were fine, in my heart I felt something was going to happen, I just didn't know when.

The following day, Anthony went to the studio to complete the B side of his cassette. When he arrived home, handed me a copy of the A side to record along with a photo for the cover for me to have. What he didn't realize was that the picture he had given me was the wrong one. This dummy gave me a picture of him and Becky in the studio. We got into our first big argument of the New Year. That night, Anthony left because there was nothing he could really say about the photo. There's no reason why she should have been in the studio with him. Anthony and I separated that night.

It was me against the world again. Enough was enough. I was fed up with men. I did not want to even see one because I would have probably killed him. I had been back and forth with Anthony for almost eight years and could not take anymore bull from him so it was best that I departed from him for good.

A week had past, before I decided to go out and party. I made the decision to work on me so I just focused on my job and got my house in order. I did not get involved with anyone. I had issues I had to workout and besides that I had been out of the dating game in so long, I didn't know what to say to a brother. Instead, I chilled with my friends in Brooklyn and on Staten Island.

June rolled around and it was my birthday week. I had no plans. Rosie called and asked me to go over to her house to have some drinks and chill with the rest of our girlfriends. It sounded like a good idea, so I went. We drank Rum-and-Cokes and I even had some Harvey's Bristol Cream. That night, we celebrated our single status as women. We always had something to celebrate. In the 90's, we found anything to celebrate.

The next morning, my butt was sick. I was throwing up all over the place. The girls knew that if I threw up, I was not ok because I was not a drinker. I always acted like I was. That night, I had a little bit too much fun. I got so sick, I had to go to the hospital. Any medication given to me, I would throw up. I thought that I was just throwing up from the liquor but the doctor said, "You are in early stages of pregnancy."

I asked, "Early like?"

"Four weeks."

Rosie was with me and said, "You'll never get rid of Anthony now!"

I said, "You must be crazy."

Rosie said, "Are you going to tell him."

"I don't know," I replied. "I don't want him to think that I was trying to keep him so I may just have my baby without him knowing."

Rosie said, "So you want to raise a baby by yourself? Fita we were blessed. We have both of our parents and now you are going to raise your child without a father."

"Rosie give me until the end of the month."

The next day, Rosie beeped Anthony and told him that I need to talk to him. Anthony then beeped me and I said, "I just wanted you to know that I'm pregnant but you can stay wherever you're at. I just wanted you to know. No, we are not getting back together and I don't need you."

Anthony said, "Are you done?"

"Yes," I replied and Anthony hung up.

One week later, someone beeped me from an unfamiliar number. I called the number back and it was a girl and she said, "So you having a baby? Are you sure it's Anthony's? How many months are you?"

I said, "WHO THE HELL IS THIS?"

The girl replied, "Who do you think it is?"

"If I knew, I would not be asking!"

"It's Becky."

"What is it your business if I'm pregnant?" I asked.

Becky said, "Well he is with me now and we live together."

"So! I don't want him."

"Well I don't think it's his."

"Well Becky, I don't have to prove anything to you."

Becky said, "Well Anthony don't think it's his either."

I said, "Becky, the hell with you and Anthony."

Before Becky could say anything else, Anthony got on the phone and said, "I was in the bathroom. What happened?"

I said, "Your girl called questioning me about the pregnancy and that you and her don't think it's yours. You don't have to call me anymore. This is my baby!" and I hung up.

The harassment between Anthony and Becky towards me continued. I was stressed and depressed. I stopped answering my telephone for a few days. The next week, I received a call from Anthony saying that he wanted to take a DNA test. Becky told him that it could not be his because the doctor told Becky that Anthony could not make any children. I screamed at Anthony and said, "You stupid fool. Don't call here anymore." My mother went upstairs to my apartment and asked me if I was alright. I told her I was fine but that I was arguing with Anthony about the baby. My mother said, "Fita just leave things alone. That girl will realize that Anthony ain't good for her. "

Everyday, there were messages sent from the both of them. It got to the point where I had changed my telephone number again. It was better that way so that I could go on with my life. I continued to rebuild my life and I started spending more time with my mother. My mom spoiled me during my pregnancy. She and I bonded from that time on. I was alone and my mother was too. My father had passed away and she never had any other male friends. It was me and my mother against all odds.

I found more fun in this pregnancy then any other. I was about eight weeks and I woke up with my bed full of blood. I can't believe this. I had miscarried in my sleep. I woke up screaming and mother ran upstairs. She looked and saw all the blood and knew what had happened. We got dressed and she took me to the hospital for me to get a DNC. I was devastated.

On my way home, I looked up to the sky and said, "I'm sorry Lord," and cried. My mother said, "It's okay. You will have a baby one day, when God is ready to give you your blessing again." I went back into depression. It was only about three months, and I really had not gotten over my father's death and now this. I began to think about my first abortion, and then my other miscarriage that caused me to go into a rage at work. I had to be sent me home on a stress leave of an accident. Thank God that I was working on Staten Island because I would have gone crazy with all of that happening to me in Brooklyn. I had to go to stress management classes with the Department of Sanitation. I called them my NA (Narcotics Anonymous) meeting.

I was not on drugs and I did not drink but I was not far from doing both those things with all that was happening. I was extremely stressed out. I ended up on leave for three months from work.

When I returned, I felt that God was giving me a fresh start so I ran with it. I got myself together and I got back on regular duty. I worked through some of the hottest days and before I realized, it was the holidays. I never forgot the holidays. It was the first holiday in a long time where I was a single woman. I had not heard from Anthony because he didn't have my number. Instead, I had seen Junie but it was not the same. We spoke and kept it moving.

It was a "new day." When Thanksgiving arrived, I enjoyed myself at my house with my family. My brother Junior and his wife Vickie and the children were with me. My niece Victoria was now 13 years old, Chino was 10 years old, and Stephanie was 7 years old. They were getting so big and I could not allow them to see foolishness. Although we laughed and played games, I still felt alone. Outwardly, I was fighting my depression.

Six months passed, and I had not seen or heard from Anthony. I was making good progress. This was the longest time that we had not been together. A few days before Christmas weekend, my house was full again. My comedian friend Derrick, boxer Mike, and a couple of music artist were waiting at my house for Rosie to arrive so we could go out clubbing. We had made arrangements to go to Atlantic City for the weekend to see Mike box. Each of us was doing big things for the holidays. The telephone rung and it was Rosie.

She said, "You need to sit down and I hope you are alone."

I said, "No everyone is here and waiting on you."

She said, "I will be there but I need to tell you this first...It's loud in your living room. Go to your room or the kitchen."

I said, "Okay!" So I didn't seem rude, I told my guest that I would be back and encouraged them to help themselves to drinks in my absence, and I went to the kitchen.

Rosie said, "Well it's about Anthony." My heart dropped.

I said, "WHAT? Rosie is he dead?"

"He might as well be."

"What happened?"

She said, "He has been calling me because you always change your number, and he said that you will probably not speak to him anymore."

I said, "What!"

Rosie said, "Anthony is locked up and he is facing life!" My mouth was on the floor and my heart was racing.

"What happened?"

"He would like to call you," she replied.

I said, "Give him my number."

"He is going to call you in about fifteen minutes."

"Okay, bring your butt on."

Rosie said, "I will be there in twenty-five minutes."

I went back into the living room and joined my guest. I tried to continue enjoying myself but my conscious was bothering me until I heard from Anthony. I did not feel good. The phone rang and I didn't hear the corrections operator on the other line so I said, "Hello!"

Anthony said, "Hello!"

"Hello Anthony!"

"How are you," he asked.

I said, "Fine." I then told Anthony hold on. I needed to go into another room.

Anthony said, "Am I disturbing you?"

"No, it's the holidays and I have company."

"Your new man?"

"No, that's Derrick."

Anthony said, "Fat Derrick the comedian?"

I said, "Yes!"

"How is the baby in the stomach? You should be about ready to go in."

I said, "No Anthony, I lost the baby after all the harassment from you and Becky. It was about a month later when my mother took me to the hospital. I had a break down afterward and I was out of work for three months on a stress leave from the department." "No....No....!" He replied.

I said, "No what?"

"I'm so sorry if I caused you to lose the baby."

"No, maybe God doesn't want me to have your child."

"That's not true. You are going to have my baby."

I said, "Whatever! Anthony, where are you?"

He said, "Down the block."

"Stop lying!"

"I'm at home."

I replied, "Let me hear your demo."

Anthony said, "I don't have it. It's in the studio." He did not know that Rosie had already told me that he was locked up.

"How is Becky?"

Anthony said, "I guess she is fine."

I asked, "You are not with her?"

"No."

"Anthony, what did you call me for?"

"I just wanted to hear your voice and see how you were doing."

"Anthony what is wrong? It sounds quiet."
Anthony said, "I really miss you and I'm sorry."
I said, "You miss me now. Why, cause you are locked up?"
"So Rosie told you?"
"Yes. What happened?"
"I don't want to talk about it."
I said, "Okay, well Anthony I have company but if you like you can call me if you need to talk."
Anthony said, "Thanks! Take care."
I hung up and my heart was in pain. I knew that I would not ever see him again. I went back to the living room with and joined my guest when Rosie rang the doorbell. When I opened the door for Rosie to enter, she asked if Anthony had called and I said yes. She noticed that I was not up for partying but it was planned so she helped me get in the mood.

We both went upstairs to my apartment and drank. After a couple of shots, of I don't know what, we went downstairs to inform everyone that it was time to go. We all put on our coats and headed to Bay Street on Staten Island.

It was about 2:00 a.m. and we were all bombed. We decided to leave Bay Street and go to *Perkins* to eat breakfast. I ordered a cup of coffee for starters, and french toast with bacon. Rosie had ham and eggs with home fries, and Derrick had a cheeseburger deluxe. After we ate, we left and went our separate ways. Rosie and I went to my house and Derrick went to his.

On our way home, Rosie had read my mind. She said, "You are worried about Anthony aren't you?" I said, "Yes but I am still going to Atlantic City because Mike gave us those tickets for free." Rosie said, "You are crazy!"

The next morning the phone rang and it was Anthony. This time I heard the correctional operator and I pressed one and accepted the collect call.

"Good Morning!" said Anthony.
I said, "Morning!"
"Are you going out?" he asked.
I said, "I'm on my way to Atlantic City to see a fight."
"Okay! When can I call you?"
"I will be gone until after Christmas."
"You going by yourself?"
"No, with Rosie."
Rosie got on the phone and said, "Hi Anthony!"
He said, "Hello Rosie! Thank you!"

She said, "You're welcome!"

"Well I will call you on the weekend."

I said, "Okay."

Rosie and I got our things together for the two day trip and bounced. As we drove through New Jersey, I could not get my mind off of Anthony. I told Rosie that I didn't want to stay after the fight. She knew how I was feeling so she didn't mind going back home. Rosie and I watched the fight. Mike won and left before the celebration.

The next morning, I got up early and took Rosie home. Later, I went to Rikers Island to give Anthony a surprise visit. Anthony was very surprised to see me.

He said, "I thought you were in Atlantic City."

I said, "I did go but I could not stay. I needed to see you and find out what is going on and how you are up in this place again. And Rosie said you may be facing life."

"God must love you," he said.

"Why you say that?"

He said, "Every time I get in an argument with you, something happens."

I said, "That's because you say things and you think your stuff don't stink."

"That same week that we got into it, I went to my parole and there was someone that pointed me out as Divine's shooter."

"So YOU killed Divine that night you left me in the house?"

Anthony said, "I don't want to talk about it."

I said, "If you don't want to talk about it now, when are you going to talk about it with me? I was the cause."

"What's mine is mine and Divine knew that he was in violation."

I had finally gotten my answer. Anthony and I talked about the years of our lives together and most of the incidents we both laughed at. It was a good visit and I told Anthony that I would give him a visit from time to time. He said he would like that and that he appreciated me, "Ms. McEachin."

Right before the visit was over, Anthony asked, "May I have a kiss?" I said, "Yes!" and we kissed and I left. The next day, Anthony called and we talked on the telephone. I didn't visit again until after the New Year.

Chapter XIV

The Intelligent

It was January 1994, and Anthony was locked up. I decided to go visit him in prison since we remained friends and because I knew that he needed someone to spend time with. He knew that he could trust me. He finally realized that I had been a trooper all of these years. It's sometimes hard for a man to realize when they have a woman that's a ride or die chick. Anthony needed me so we went to work.

I knew the business and he had the connects. Anthony needed a paid lawyer to fight his case so he needed to make some cash. Anthony always knew how to get money wherever he was. He called his connects and set things up so that I picked up the packages. I even bagged them and Anthony had a few girls that I would give product too for them to take to him. This was the routine for about six months. I had some pull in the correctional facility. I knew some girls that had been correction officers in the jail. We had it made for a while, enough to make money for a real lawyer. In addition to moving weight, I pawned a couple of my chains and his jewelry to pull things through.

By the court date, I had hired a paid lawyer. The lawyer had already told me that he could cut a deal to get Anthony down for 7 to 14 years oppose to 15 to life. I thought it was a good idea but Anthony wanted to take it to trail. I asked, "Why would you take it to trail? If you blow trail, you will never see the streets again." Anthony did not want to face the fact that this was his life for real. Anthony stayed depressed most of the time after we worked so hard for the money in order to get the lawyer. I don't know if it was because he had fallen in love with me again or if he was afraid that I would leave him. What he did know was that if I was going to leave him, I would have never gone to see him in jail again.

The day of trail, I listened to Divine's mother disrespect my man saying how she prayed that someone killed Anthony in prison. All of what she was saying made me sick. I started to cry. She described how she found her son. With each remark, I had gotten sicker and sicker. I couldn't help to think how I would feel if it was my son but I tried to stay firm since it was my man's life on the line.

I was glad for recess. It was so hard for me to go through the trail but it was my nature to be strong. I went to lunch and following the short recess, the judge changed the court date until after the 4th of July. It was postponed because Divine's mother could not attend the second half of the day's trail.

On July 10, 1994 at 9:00 a.m., I was waiting in the court room. After waiting patiently for three hours, the meet was postponed. Anthony had a fight on the inmate bus so the court date was changed again to July 25th.

Then on the 25th of July, there was another postponement. This time Anthony cut someone on the bus. I found myself back in the court room on August 5th to find out what? It was postponed again (Of course it was). Anthony didn't know how to act. I asked the correction officer why and he said, "The nigger cut someone on the bus again." I was taken back. Not by the Anthony's actions but the fact that the Caucasian correctional officer called him a nigger right to my face.

As I was leaving the court house, I could not believe what had been happening. Everything was becoming so overwhelming for me. I would have to travel from Staten Island all the way to Queens. It was a along and difficult trip. I wasn't driving. I had to catch the bus, to the ferry, and then onto a train and then walked. The trip would get would anyone tired. I didn't drive because there was never any parking near the court house.

After all of the postponements, I went to see Anthony. I asked, "What is going on?" He said, "It was some people on the bus, so you know Fita I'm no punk and I will get a nigga' before he will get me." I sighed. Anthony asked me if I wanted to start our relationship over and I said ok but didn't think anything of it. I just agreed so that he would act right and we could finish our conversation, and figure out the court situation. But it was different for Anthony. He started getting serious after that day.

Anthony began sending me stuff at home and wiring money. When I cooked, he would have C.O's (Correction Officers) from Staten Island pick-up his dinner from me. He wanted my cooking. Who wouldn't when you're in prison? Regardless, I thought it was sweet. It kind of seemed like he was home. I told Anthony that I wanted him to act right and get his self together. Of course, I've been saying that since 1984. September 10, 1994 was Anthony's chance. It was the last court date and the court said that if he was not going to get sentenced that day, they would make sure that the 7-14 year bid would be the only offer on the table.

Thank God Anthony did make it. The correction officer walked him into the court room. I didn't know how to feel. The officer then took the shackles off his legs and hands, and that's when I started to cry. The judge proceeded to say, "Anthony your sentence will be 7 to 14 years." I began to scream. I couldn't compose myself. I thought I was prepared but when you hear something like that, you just don't know how you're going to react. The thought of him being away for 7 to 14 years was disheartening.

Anthony and I looked at each other, and he asked, "Are you going to wait?" I didn't reply. Instead, my tears began to roll faster and faster down my face as if they were racing each other. I think my heart even skipped a beat. I thought I was going to die. Anthony's lawyer had to pick me up off the ground. The sentence was delivered and the love of my life was going away for a long, long, long time.

Immediately after Anthony was sentenced to Rikers Island, I went to see him. He wasn't going to be sent upstate for another six months. I was happy to know that I would have some time with him.

I began seeing Anthony at least three times a week. I put money in his account, and took him clothes and food packages. We would speak a lot about our relationship and how he was shocked that the more he kept the business away from me and our home, I would know more than he thought.

"I learned from the best. My father and my man," I said. Anthony laughed.

Then he asked, "Are you going to do this time with me?"

I said, "Are you asking me to take this long ride?"

"Yes!"

"I refuse to do this without being your wife."

Anthony grinned and said, "I'm glad you said that. Here are the papers."

Anthony passed me a set of papers and I said, "Are you asking to marry me?"

"Yes, but I didn't know if you would under these circumstances.

"You deserve a big church wedding."

"If I didn't love you unconditionally, I would have left you here."

Anthony said, "My mother was right all along."

A month had passed, and I was back and forth with getting various paperwork approved for Anthony and our marriage certificate. Between working, visiting Antony throughout the week, and trying to get things settled to make our marriage official, it was exhausting. This went on until about the first of the year.

Visiting Anthony wasn't easy either. I had to stand on line for three hours for a one hour visit. The only good thing was that I had a lot of girlfriends that were correction officers that worked in the visiting room so my visits were two hours long, sometime three.

Finally by February, all the paperwork was done for our marriage but then I had to wait on an official response. During the waiting process, I still met with connects and was still picking up money in the bathrooms of the correctional facility, and in the store on Queens Blvd. Everyone knew I was Anthony's girl and they did not want any problems. Therefore, no one messed with me.

During the month of March, Anthony and I tried to make the best of the situation. We had a lot of fun by enjoying our relationship as much as possible while we waited on the approval for our special day that only God could grant us in order to join as one. On one particular visit, I remembered Anthony got on the visit with a cheesy smile. I instantly knew that he had received the paperwork back for our wedding date. The date was scheduled for April 10, 1995. That was a day that Anthony would never forget. It was his baby brother Teron's Birthday (what a coincidence).

Two days before my wedding day, I decided not to visit Anthony but instead I went to my friend's house. I needed to find a dress and get my hair done. I decided on a beige and green dress with spaghetti straps, and a pair of beige sandals to match. I didn't want to spend money on a big gown. The wedding was going to be very small and informal.

After I had covered everything, I didn't feel well. I got very ill and had to go to the hospital. Anthony was going crazy when he found out. I was hospitalized for a severe migraine headache. My head was pounding. I felt weak, dizzy, and light-headed from using over the counter products to help cure my pain. It was so bad that doctors gave me morphine, which put me to sleep.

At about 3:00 a.m., I woke up and I asked the maintenance man what time is was. I then asked the date and he said it was April 10, 1995. I sat up in my bed and said, "Oh my God! I'm getting married today," but I laid back down and feel back to sleep. I woke back up 7:00 a.m.

and was discharged from the hospital; not because doctors wanted to let me go but I told them I was getting married. I also told the doctor about the maintenance man I spoke with and the doctor said that maintenance does not work in the middle of the night on the floor that I was on. I'm sure my doctor thought I was crazy. Looking back on the incident, I think that my deceased father had come to me to wake me up for my wedding day.

When I arrived home, I rushed to get ready. I didn't have anyone to help me because my mother was in Puerto Rico and my mother-in-law, to be, was in Maryland. It was just me and my husband-to-be against the world, in unity, and as one. I was set to get married at 10:00 a.m. in the chapel of C-95 in Rikers Island Correctional Facility.

I was at Queens Blvd by 8:30 a.m., waiting on the Rikers Island bus to arrive but it didn't get there until 10:30 a.m. I panicked. My wedding was supposed to begin at 10:00 a.m. By the time I got to my wedding, I was one hour late. Anthony thought I stood him up but he still had hope. When I arrived, he was standing at the alter. Anthony recognized me and smiled. He was extremely happy to see me. He picked me up and said, "I do," to the Pastor.

The Pastor began the formal wedding ceremony. When it got to the section of the wedding vows, we recited our own. "You may kiss your bride," the Pastor said and we passionately kissed.

The correction officer stationed in the chapel tapped Anthony on the shoulder and said, "I will give you and your new bride ten minutes." I was now Mrs. Rafaela Barbour.

TO BE CONTINUED

Breinigsville, PA USA
13 September 2010
245236BV00001B/19/P